Traveling Across

America

Genevieve Welsh Bottorff

LifeRich
PUBLISHING®

This book is a work of non-fiction. Unless otherwise noted, the author
and the publisher make no explicit guarantees as to the accuracy of
the information contained in this book and in some cases, names of
people and places have been altered to protect their privacy.

LifeRich Publishing is a registered trademark of
The Reader's Digest Association, Inc.

LifeRich Publishing books may be ordered through booksellers or by contacting:

LifeRich Publishing
1663 Liberty Drive
Bloomington, IN 47403
www.liferichpublishing.com
1 (888) 238-8637

Because of the dynamic nature of the Internet, any web addresses or
links contained in this book may have changed since publication and
may no longer be valid. The views expressed in this work are solely those
of the author and do not necessarily reflect the views of the publisher,
and the publisher hereby disclaims any responsibility for them.

Any people depicted in stock imagery provided by Getty Images are
models, and such images are being used for illustrative purposes only.
Certain stock imagery © Getty Images.

ISBN: 978-1-4897-1665-1 (sc)
ISBN: 978-1-4897-1664-4 (e)

Library of Congress Control Number: 2018903792

Print information available on the last page.

LifeRich Publishing rev. date: 07/24/2018

Acknowledgements

I would like to thank and especially acknowledge our daughter, Genny, and her husband, Eric; our granddaughter, Ashley, and her husband, Eric; and our dear friends, Marge and Bob. They made this trip several years earlier. Listening to their stories of what they saw, what they did, and their adventures, lit a spark in Jim and me. These three special couples gave us the desire and a thirst to follow in their footsteps. Thank you for your inspiration.

I would also like to make a very special acknowledgement and thank you to our granddaughter, Katherine Marie. One day when we were talking, I told her that I always wanted to write a book. In her wonderful 13-year old wisdom, she said, "You should do it Granny. You will never know unless you try." You gave me the push I needed, Katie. Thank you for your wisdom and for believing in me.

Thank you, also, to my dearest and long-time friend, Donna, for your excellent proof reading skills. You were a wonderful help.

Dedication

This book is dedicated to my husband, Jim. Were it not for your encouragement, support, and love, this book would not have come to fruition. Also, were it not for your quest to seek the largest and the out of the ordinary, our trip would not have been as much fun or this book so enjoyable to write. You are my joy. You enhance my happiness.

Grow old with me, my love, the best is yet to be!

Contents

Prologue

I have always wanted to see the United States. It has been my dream for as long as I can remember. My husband, Jim, shared my dream. It took us a long time to reach the point where we could just get in the car and travel, but as soon as the opportunity opened for us, that is exactly what we did.

We had seen all of the states on the East Coast, some of the states on the West Coast, but we had not seen any of the states in the middle of the country. We knew that Mt. Rushmore was our destination and tracked a route through Middle America that would take us there. We had no set plan other than that we did not want to go on major roads. We wanted to see the small towns and countryside that made up this great country.

Jim and I did some research on the states we wanted to see, but other than that, we followed our own direction. We would get up in the morning, get in the car, and go. We had an idea of where we wanted to go and what we wanted to see, but if something more interesting piqued our curiosity, we detoured and went to see it. We were always glad we followed our instincts. They led us to interesting places we would never have known.

We had no set plan of where we would stay except for when we stayed at one of our timeshares. At the end of the day, we would check into a hotel, get some sleep, and eagerly look forward to where the next day would take us.

After raising four children and working since we were 18, this was a life of total freedom. It was most enjoyable. We would do it again in a heartbeat. When we are too old to go anywhere, we can sit in our rocking chairs and remember all the wonderful things we saw and the great times we had along the way.

If you have ever wanted to take a trip like this, I encourage you to do it. If it is not something you can do right now, make plans to do it another time. You will not regret it. This is one of the best things we ever did for us. The sights you will see, the places you will go, along with finally having the time for each other and discovering each other again after years spent building your family and home, is joy that cannot be equaled.

We invite you to come along with us on this journey. We would love to have your company.

Enjoy!

Chapter 1

After a fun-filled week with our grandchildren in Virginia, we are beginning one of our dreams – a road trip across America.

We were in Virginia to stay with our granddaughter, Delaney, while her parents, Jim and Jeannine, went away. We had a great time being with her. We even got to see her Band Concert. That was quite a thrill. Living in Florida, it is not something we get to do often.

We have two grandsons, Lucas and Andrew, who live close by in Virginia and we got to be with them, also. We went to Andrew's Little League baseball game. That was fun. After the game, we took all three children to dinner and to see the movie, "Maleficent." The movie was good. It wasn't scary like I thought it would be. From there, all three grandchildren had a sleepover with us. That was so much fun.

Delaney asked me what the best thing was that I did while I was there. I told her it was the sleepover, followed by her concert, Andrew's baseball game, teaching Lucas how to make something, telling stories, and seeing their happy smiling faces. Being with them was the best way to start a vacation.

After leaving our family, we spent the night in Lexington, VA. It was a stormy night and we were happy to get off the road. The morning dawned sunny and beautiful as we made our way to West Virginia. Of course, we sang, "Take Me Home, Country Roads," as we drove through West Virginia. John Denver and his songs were, are, and always will be my favorites. It just wouldn't have been right not to sing that great song while we were going through West Virginia.

Our first stop was The Greenbrier in White Sulphur Springs, West Virginia, an historic inn that dates back to the 1700's. It was totally awesome! I have never seen such grandeur. It certainly didn't look like that in the 1700's. The Greenbrier Inn is a huge, sprawling white hotel with red awnings, surrounded by large trees and beautiful flowering gardens. The red awnings stood out so well against the white hotel. We went inside and the inside was magnificent. Words don't come close to describing how beautiful it was. On the bottom floor of the hotel were shops. There was a toy store grander than any toy store I have ever seen. I walked around wide-eyed looking at the toys. The restaurant was on the main floor. It looked like the first-class dining room on the Titanic. It was breath-taking with chandeliers sparkling all over the room. There were many other rooms (sitting rooms, parlors, libraries) on the first floor, each one decorated differently, one grander than the other.

The Greenbrier is a four seasons resort. There are also cottages, pools, a championship golf course, ski area, activities for children, and activities for adults. The hotel was incredible in every way. In case you are interested, you can buy a home on their grounds for one million dollars, and enjoy it every day.

A very interesting fact about The Greenbrier is that it was used as a bunker for our government in the event of an emergency. Under the hotel were all the facilities needed to protect and run the government.

From great opulence, we took the back road through West Virginia and saw how the other half lives. We did not want to stay on interstates on this trip. We wanted to see the byways. The road took us through the mountains. The mountains were beautiful, lush, and very green. We saw modest houses, trailers, and some not-so-nice houses, but mostly modest houses. There were small villages spread throughout the mountains. A sign posted the name of the village and underneath the name was the word, "Unincorporated."

I didn't know what that meant, so I asked. It means that they don't have a local government.

On the top of the mountain, the temperature was around 65 degrees. In the valley, the temperature was around 85 degrees – quite a difference. The road was very winding.. It wound around the mountains, up and down. Sometimes I felt like I was on a roller coaster. I was glad when we got off that road, but also glad that I got to experience it.

When we came down from the mountains, we were in a valley of small coal, steel, and manufacturing towns with names like Alloy, Smithers, Rainelle, and Rupert. In Rainelle, we had to wait for a train to go by before we could continue. It was a long train with car after car filled with coal. I was amazed to see so many coal collieries. Each town had one. Alloy is a metallurgical coal town.

The collieries weren't much different from the collieries in my grandfather's time, only slightly improved. The whole area would remind you of the coal towns in Pennsylvania. Riding from town to town, I almost expected to see the town of Jim Thorpe around the bend. I felt very much at home in this area. The houses looked like the houses in coal towns in Northeast Pennsylvania. Some of them were big and very nice. I knew them to be the mine owner's homes. I had no trouble recognizing the coal miner's homes. They were small and not so nice.

The town of Smithers really rated. They had a McDonald's. I happily got my caramel frappe and we continued on to Charleston, the capitol of West Virginia.

Charleston was a very nice city. The Capitol Building was beautiful. The gold dome was outstanding. I could see it from far away. Charleston reminded me of Philadelphia and Pittsburgh. Fraternity and sorority houses, along with a Boat House Row, lined the Kanawha River, just as they did the Schuylkill River in Philadelphia. Mountains, a river, and old bridges surrounded Charleston, just as they did in Pittsburgh. We saw the University of Charleston and many of the huge old homes in the town. They were beautiful.

Leaving Charleston, we continued on to Huntington, the home of Marshall University. We loved the movie, "We Are Marshall," and wanted to see the university and the town. The movie and the courage of the people were very inspiring. It was great to see the university and the town.

We ended our day in Lexington, Kentucky. From what I've seen so far, it is beautiful; lush green grass and many horse farms. I am looking forward to seeing more tomorrow.

On this trip, we are planning to drive through the middle states and up to South Dakota. We will return to Pennsylvania driving through the northern states. There should be lots of fun and interesting things to see along the way.

Me – I can't wait to see Mt. Rushmore. Jim – he can't wait to see the largest ball of twine. That's us! Let the journey begin.

West Virginia　**The Mountain State**
State Motto – "Mountaineers are Always Free"
License Plate Saying – Mountain State

Chapter 2

We spent a great day in Lexington, Kentucky. Lexington is beautiful. The houses are still the big, old, beautiful homes they once were. I love the wrap-around porches, columns, and upstairs balconies. Many of the houses were made of brick. Bricks were more durable, but were expensive, keeping them in the realm of the wealthy.

Our first stop was the Mary Todd Lincoln House in downtown Lexington. It goes back to the 1800's and was once an inn. Mary's father purchased the house in the 1832. There were 16 children in the Todd family. Two of the children died as infants. This house is where Mary grew up. The house has been refurbished and was beautifully decorated with many of the original Todd and Lincoln furnishings. Mary's porcelain collection was prominent in each room.

There were 14 rooms in the house. As you walked into the house, you entered the foyer. There were steps to the back of the foyer, leading to the upstairs. A family parlor was on the right followed by the dining room, eating room for the children, and the kitchen. On the left was the guest parlor. The guest parlor was very large and took up the whole left side of the downstairs. Upstairs on the left was the master bedroom with a nursery. The children's playroom followed. There was also another bedroom on the left side. Across the hall were two other bedrooms. On the third floor was a big bedroom for the boys in the family. President Lincoln, Mary, and their family stayed in this house at one point. It was an absolute thrill to be there, especially when the tour guide said, "Lincoln held onto this railing when he went up the stairs." I made sure I kept my hand on the railing all the way up to the third floor and all the way down. WOW, I had my hand on the same railing as Abraham Lincoln. Beyond thrilling!

The tour guide also told us a lot about Mary. He told us that she was treated harshly by historians. Her husband was assassinated, three of her children died, she suffered from severe migraines, and her only surviving child, Robert had her declared insane and committed her to an insane asylum. She was taking laudanum for her headaches and another drug. She was also into spiritualism. These three things combined made her act delusional. After she was committed, she stopped taking all drugs and within three months was well, declared sane, and released. She left America and went to live in France. She didn't return to America until a year before her death.

Mary never forgave her son for having her committed. She was well-educated and spoke fluent French. She came from a wealthy and privileged background. Washington society thought she was a "country bumpkin" like Lincoln. They criticized and shunned her. That, along with losing three children, her husband, and severe migraines, was enough to put anyone over the edge. I certainly can understand.

I didn't know much about Mary, except for the insanity trial, but I'm so glad I got to hear the behind-the-scenes story. Mary was a good woman, not a great woman, but one who tried to do her best for our country, and was scorned no matter what she did.

I also found it interesting that Mary and Jackie Kennedy picked the same china pattern when in the White House; they both lost children while there; and both lost their husbands to assassins while they were in office.

After leaving the Mary Todd Lincoln House, we went to the Town Branch Brewery and Distillery. It is one of four distilleries in our country that brew both beer and bourbon. First, we watched a movie about the distillery. I found it informative. This was a very productive and active brewery from the 1700's until Prohibition in the 1900's. The owners were arrested for bootlegging during Prohibition and the brewery was closed. The brewery that exists today was begun by a gentleman who came from Ireland in 1976 and settled in Kentucky. His name was Pearce Lyons.

I never knew how beer or bourbon was made and we were shown a video about how they are made. I found it very interesting. After the movie, we moved on to the beer processing plant and the tasting. At Town Branch, they make six different beers. I am not a beer drinker, but I tried two. The first was a peach ale. They actually use peach slices in the processing. I did like that beer and could get used to drinking peach ale. The other was a bourbon beer. The beer is aged in bourbon barrels. That tasted good, too. From there we went to the bourbon distillery and tasting. I could actually see the bourbon fermenting in huge tanks. I could feel the heat from the yeast, see it bubbling, and the smell was wonderful. I tried bourbon and it was so strong, it took my breath away. I couldn't drink that.

One of the best drinks I tasted was Mr. Lyons' version of Irish coffee. He created his version as a bourbon coffee liquor. It was in a fancy bottle like Bailey's and was thick like syrup. The guide poured a little into a glass, followed by boiling hot water, and then cold heavy cream. The result was delicious! I drank all of my sample and really liked it. I learned a lot at this brewery and just might change my drinking habits.

We saw many horse farms with lush green grass surrounded by fences. We were amazed by the fences. There were so many of them. We saw so much today, and the best was yet to be.

A woman at the Visitors' Center told us not to miss Claudia Sanders' restaurant. Claudia was the wife of Colonel Sanders, of Kentucky Fried Chicken fame. We didn't know the restaurant existed. She told us a funny story about when she went there. She told us that she and her friends pulled into the wrong driveway. They pulled into Colonel Sanders' driveway, not the restaurant driveway. She said that Colonel Sanders came out, greeted them, and escorted them to the restaurant. She said that he was so nice.

We traveled on to Shelbyville and found Claudia Sanders restaurant. We stopped for dinner there. The restaurant was huge, with many very nice dining rooms. The menu offered a lot of great choices, but we settled on the fried chicken. I am not a big Kentucky Fried Chicken fan, mostly because I don't like fast food, but this fried chicken was different and very delicious. The dinner came with soup, salad, fried chicken, potatoes, rolls, and vegetables. All were delicious. Jim and I enjoyed every morsel and felt really special being in Claudia Sanders restaurant. Funny what you can see and do in America when you get off the big highways and try the backroads.

We are now settled in for the night in Louisville, Kentucky, and are looking forward to exploring Louisville tomorrow. We are also planning to have dinner with our friends, Larry, and his wife, Mary. Larry went to elementary school with us at Immaculate Conception Grade School in the Germantown section of Philadelphia. We are really looking forward to seeing them.

I don't know, between the brewery and the fried chicken, Jim forgot about the largest ball of twine. We'll see if he remembers tomorrow. Me – I haven't forgotten Mt. Rushmore. Can't wait!

Chapter 3

WOW, you will never believe where I was today! I was at Churchill Downs in Louisville, Kentucky, sitting in the stands, watching the Belmont Stakes on their giant TV's. Beyond exciting! As the race began, everyone stood up and started chanting, "Chrome, Chrome, Chrome." Of course, it was disappointing when Chrome didn't win, but it was exciting to be there and be a part of the event.

Churchill Downs is huge and beautiful. It was packed with people for race day. I saw many fancy hats and many people beautifully dressed. It was cool to see. Some people were dressed in shorts and sneakers, but that was not the norm. It is true what you read about race day – most people go all out, wearing great hats and very nice attire. When I started this day, I never dreamed I would be at Churchill Downs. It was really fun.

Jim and I started the day at the Louisville Slugger Museum where they make the famous Louisville Slugger baseball bats. We actually went into the factory and watched the bats being made. I learned a lot. The bats are made of ash or maple wood. When you are watching a baseball game and the bat breaks, it is made of maple. If the bat splinters, it is made of ash.

It used to take 30 minutes to hand carve the bats. With the machines of today, a bat can be carved in 30 seconds. The company makes one million eight hundred thousand bats a year. When the bats come off the carving machine, they have nubs at each end. They go on to the sanding machine and the machine holds the bat by the nubs while it sands. The nubs are then broken off by the machine. From the sanding machine, the bat goes to the firing station to be branded with the company name. The finished bat is beautiful and is used by all major baseball teams. The company that makes the Louisville Slugger Bats is Hillerich and Bradsby. They have been making them since 1856. We were given tiny finished bats to keep and we could also keep the nubs that were broken off by the machine. I made sure I got some for my grandchildren. I know they will like them.

After learning how the bats are made, we went into the baseball museum. We watched a movie called, "It's All in The Crack of the Bat." It was interesting, as were the various displays of major league baseball players and baseball games. The museum covered players from the beginning of baseball. It also covered the time when there were women baseball leagues during World War II. The museum was very interesting. I just might become a baseball fan.

Louisville has a street fair called "Fourth Street Live." One of the main streets is blocked off solely for entertainment. It is much like Fremont Street in Las Vegas. The locals come for the day with their coolers, food, and chairs. The restaurants were open for business, even the bars, and we were there around noon. We walked around for a while, then stopped to watch a pole vaulting competition. There were many competitors – all fit and eager to try their hand at pole vaulting. At night, there are lights all around the street and there is music and dancing. Everyone seemed to be enjoying the day. It looked like a great way to spend a Sunday. We enjoyed seeing it and being a part of it.

We then drove around the city, saw some of the sights, and even crossed the bridge into Indiana. The downtown area of Louisville is very nice. There were only four skyscrapers. Not many large buildings at all. We drove down Mohammed Ali Street. We saw the football stadium that Papa John Pizza built for the University of Louisville. We also saw the KFC Yum! Center. It is a basketball sports center and the third largest college arena in the U.S., also built for the University of Louisville. Yum! Brands Inc. include Taco Bell, KFC, Pizza Hut, and Wing Street.

We went to Union Station, Louisville's old train station. We drove by it and, at first, I thought it was a church because it had so many steeples. Then, I saw the Union Station sign on the front of the building. Of course, we had to go into the station. It was magnificent! The outside was beautiful, but the inside was spectacular. There were rows and rows of beautiful mahogany train seats for waiting passengers, mahogany wood throughout the building, awesome stained-glass windows, and the ceiling was completely stained glass. I am so glad we stopped and went inside. The station is now being used as a center for children and for adult education.

I am so proud of Louisville for preserving a treasure of the past. Today too many things, rich in history and culture, get torn down, robbing future generations of the joy and privilege of learning about the past.

The best thing about this day was being with our friend, Larry, and meeting his wife, Mary. Larry and Mary live in the historic district of Old Louisville. Their home is beautiful from the outside and even more beautiful inside. They have kept the ambiance of the day with the original hardwood floors, fireplaces, crown molding, and some of the stained-glass windows. The fireplaces were outlined in wood and had double mantles. A double mantle means that it has two shelves instead of one.

Larry and Mary have a beautiful garden in the back of their home. The garden has a lovely water fountain, trees, a brick walkway, and many varieties of flowers. Every year Louisville has a Garden Tour, and their garden was featured in the tour last year. It was a delight seeing their home and how they have preserved the beauty of the house.

The four of us went for a walk through the historic district and Larry and Mary showed us a lot of other historic houses. They were so big, beautiful and, again, built of brick. I could just imagine all the parties and balls that were held in them and picture the horse-drawn carriages bringing women in their magnificent gowns to the ball. Some of the houses had horseshoe steps. They are steps with a curved railing going up each side. The men went up one side of the steps and the women went up the other side. This was necessary so that when the ladies lifted their gowns to go up the steps, the men wouldn't be able to see their ankles or legs. They were the mores of that time!

It was great seeing Larry again and getting to meet Mary. We had a wonderful day with them. They took us to Churchill Downs. We had dinner there and had a great time talking, sharing stories of our school days, and laughing together. They both look wonderful. Life in Louisville agrees with them. Actually, Larry and I go way back, from toddlers to teens and continuing to adults. He was my neighbor on Woodstock Street in my old neighborhood before we moved. We still remember going together to Mrs. Dear's store for penny candy. No one had a phone in their house in those days. Her store had the only phone in the neighborhood. If there was an emergency, family knew to call Mrs. Dear's store. She would come and get whomever the call was for, and we talked on her phone. That's how it was in the "olden days." Anyway, Jim and I can't thank Larry and Mary enough for sharing their Saturday with us.

So, being in Kentucky, I learned that the state is famous for its bourbon, blue grass, baseball bats, and horses. Things I didn't know before visiting this state.

Tomorrow we are off to St. Louis, Missouri. You bet we're going to get our picture taken at the Arch. Jim told me today that the largest ball of twine is in Kansas. He's waiting! Me -- I continue to look forward to seeing Mt. Rushmore. Stay tuned!

Kentucky   The Bluegrass State
           State Motto – "United We Stand, Divided We Fall"
           License Plate Saying – Bluegrass State

Chapter 4

Today, I crossed the "Mighty Mississippi" and the "Wide Missouri," both while going into St. Louis. The Missouri is wide. I didn't see the Mississippi, though. I was too busy trying to take a picture of the Arch. The Arch is huge! It is the size of skyscrapers. You see it long before you reach the city. I spotted it from way back. We didn't go to the Arch today, but we will get there tomorrow. I can't wait to see it and get pictures. Tomorrow will be our day to explore St. Louis. I'll make sure I see the Mississippi, too.

On the way to St. Louis, we drove through some of Indiana and Illinois. From the highway, what we saw of those states was beautiful. Both are very flat, but rich in grass and trees; very good farmland. That is what we saw mostly, farm after farm; beautiful, well taken care of, and very large.

We are staying outside of St. Louis in St. Charles. St. Charles was the first capitol of Missouri. It was built along the Missouri River and was the last "civilized" stop by the Lewis and Clark Expedition. We drove through the historic district. It was beautiful and so original. We were on Main Street and I could easily picture ships in the river, horse-drawn wagons on the street, even covered wagons going through the town on their way out west.

Once again, the houses and buildings were made of brick; even the main street and sidewalks were brick. The interesting thing about the houses was that not only did they have front porches, but also side and back porches. Each floor of the house had its own porch.

On the back of the house, the porch faced the Missouri River. It must have been incredible back then to sit on those porches, gaze at the river, watch the ships come in, see people from all over coming and going, and feel the cool breezes from the river. Sounds idyllic! Tomorrow we will explore more of St. Charles.

Before we left Florida, I bought a small stuffed lion. I named her Maggie. When you squeeze her stomach, she roars. As I am sure you know, riding in a car for a long time can get tiring and one can get testy. I got Maggie to keep Jim and me in line. When I drive him crazy, he can squeeze Maggie and let me know. When he drives me crazy, I can do the same. I am happy to report that Maggie has only roared twice since we started this trip. Pretty good start!

Today was spent mostly in the car driving from Kentucky to Missouri. It was overcast the whole way, with ashen skies, so it was a good day to sit back and just ride. We stayed on the highways, except to get off once for a frappe for me.

While we were stopped at McDonald's for the frappe, we saw this beautiful building sitting on top of a hill. We decided to check it out. The building turned out to be the Immaculate Conception Monastery in Ferdinand, Indiana. The outside building was so beautiful, of course, we had to go inside. We had the most wonderful and incredible experience while there.

We were greeted by a nun who warmly welcomed us. Jim and I went to Immaculate Conception School in Philadelphia, PA, our parish in Jim Thorpe, PA is the Immaculate Conception, and we find the Immaculate Conception Monastery – and on Pentecost. What are the chances of that happening? This was not a coincidence! Sister showed us around and told us about the monastery. It has been a monastery since the 1700's, not in its present state, but an operating monastery has been on that site for a very long time. Inside and outside the monastery was incredibly beautiful. It sat high on a hill, overlooking the valley. The monastery encompassed many acres of ground, with several buildings for future sisters. They have about 120 women in the process of becoming nuns right now. It is run by the Benedictine sisters and is one of the largest communities in the United States.

Jim and I went into the church to say a prayer. It is an old Irish custom to make three wishes when you go to a church you have never been before. We made sure we did that. We knelt there for a while, enjoying the peace and beauty of the church. It was a special moment, made more special because we were experiencing it together.

Before we left, we said goodbye to Sister. I took her hands and thanked her for welcoming us. She prayed with us that we would have many of God's blessings on our journey and that we would be safe. Being me, of course I cried. She was so kind to us. I felt like I had taken a step back in time to my roots and it felt very good.

When we got in the car, Jim and I looked at each other and said, "That was a holy place. We were standing on holy ground." This visit to Immaculate Conception Monastery was such a beautiful, incredible, spiritual experience. Mere words are not adequate. I will carry this day with me always. God is so good!

Jim has now decided that along with the largest ball of twine, he also wants to see the largest pencil. Wonder what else he can come up with?! Me – Crazy Horse is waiting, close to Mt. Rushmore.

Chapter 5

Oh my gosh, you cannot imagine how incredible it was to go up in the Arch, "The Gateway to the West." The Arch is so big inside that there are museums, movies, all kinds of things to see. I was so excited just to be there, just to see it; I didn't know there was more. You can actually ride up to the top of the Arch! I don't like heights and, at first, I wasn't going to do it, but changed my mind. I asked myself, "When are you going to be here to do this again? Carpe Diem!" I wasn't going to miss this opportunity.

The Arch is huge. I took a picture of it and the top of it was in the clouds. It is majestic, towering above the other buildings in the skyline of St. Louis. It is the first thing you see when you catch sight of the city. It stands almost on the banks of the Mississippi. The inside is very impressive. You wouldn't know you were standing in the Arch, there is so much to see.

The tram that takes you to the top is inside the Arch. It's not like a tram that you ride in Disney World. It is a very small, enclosed, safe car. It takes four minutes to get to the top and three minutes to get back down. As I said, I wasn't going to go to the top, especially when I saw this small car, but I told myself that I could handle seven minutes. I thought the tram just went up and right back down. Wrong, at the top you get out. I wasn't going to do that either, but I had to because the tram was going back down to pick up other people. I was fine on the tram and I was fine at the top, too. The ride on the tram was simple and easy. My worries were for naught.

At the top of the Arch, you can look out over the whole city. There are windows on the sides. The view was so beautiful – breathtaking! I took pictures from the top, LOVED the whole experience, and wouldn't have missed it for the world.

After viewing the top for a while, we got on the tram and went back down. Once back down, we chose to visit the museum. I could have stayed there all day. Anyone who knows me and museums, that is exactly what I would have done. The Arch is called "The Gateway to the West," because anyone going to the West had to pass through St. Louis to get there. The Arch was built to honor Thomas Jefferson who was the President who made the Louisiana Purchase and commissioned Lewis and Clark to explore the territory. The museum was about the Lewis and Clark Expedition that accomplished this. There was so much to see in the museum and so much information: Excerpts from Lewis' diary, Clark's diary, notes about Sacagawea (one of their guides), pictures of the territory, artifacts, replicas of the wagons used, replicas of the animals they would have encountered, even a replica of a sod house. The exhibits/displays were so extensive. I absorbed everything!

When I was young, I always wanted to be a pioneer girl crossing the prairie. I thought it would be so exciting. I read every book I could find on the subject. I thought I knew a lot about the pioneers. I didn't! One of the guides gave a talk about the pioneers and how they crossed the country. Contrary to what we read and saw in the movies, most of the pioneers did not cross America in covered Conestoga wagons. Only a few had covered wagons. Most had a plain, medium, wooden wagon that was pulled by an ox. All their belongings were piled in the wagon. They did not ride in the wagon, they walked. They did not sleep in the wagon, they slept on the ground. An ox was used to pull the wagon because he was strong enough to do that; because he would eat the prairie grass and they wouldn't have to feed the ox; and because once they got to their destination, the ox would be used to pull the plow on the farm. There were no roads. The ride was so bumpy that the butter churn was put in the wagon and at the end of the day, the cream would be butter from being jostled so much. The washboard the women used to do their wash was also used as a musical instrument at night when they gathered around the campfire. Once the water was boiled over the fire, everyone – even children – drank coffee. The water wasn't fit to drink and had to be boiled. I learned so much listening to the guide and reading the information about the exhibits. The life that was so glamorized in the books I read and the movies I saw, wasn't so appealing to me now. There were still more exhibits and still more things to learn, but other places were beckoning.

When we left the Arch, it was mid-afternoon, just enough time to catch the last tour at Anheuser-Busch, and, of course, stop for a frappe for me. The Anheuser-Busch complex is huge. It encompasses several city blocks (142 acres) and many buildings (137). You are not going to believe this, but every building is made of brick – EVERY building!

This is a very classy brewery. I expected a factory, but it's not a factory. The railings are white wrought iron, chandeliers hang from the ceilings, and beautiful wood is evident throughout. This is not just in the Visitor's Center, this is in every building. I couldn't believe it. Throughout the complex, inside and out, are sculpted eagles and pictures of eagles. I walked around looking at the eagles and thought to myself, "Mr. Anheuser must be very patriotic." I mentioned what I thought to Jim who set me straight by telling me that eagles are the brewery's symbol. What do I know about beer?! Also, once you leave the Visitor's Center and go outside, the smell of beer is very strong. You can smell it all over, sort of like when we went to Hershey, PA and all you smell is chocolate. The tour is free and the beer samples are free. What's not to like about that?! You can even see some of the Clydesdale horses. They own 200 of them. Some are on display at the brewery, most are at their farms in Missouri, Colorado, and New Hampshire.

Again, I learned how beer is made. Budweiser is made with hops, barley, yeast, etc. but they also add rice to the mixture. It is the rice that gives Bud its crisp taste. We were in a room that was very hot from the yeast fermenting and a room that was very cold for the processing.

In the middle of the tour, we were given Bud and Bud Light to sample. The samples they gave us were in glasses, very nice glasses, not plastic or paper cups. At the end of the tour, we were also given free beer – and in glasses. I was impressed that they gave us samples in glasses. Nothing is too much for Budweiser. Jim got Shock Top. I took a taste of it and it wasn't bad. I still like the peach beer best.

Every day at 3:00 pm, the brew masters meet to taste the beer. Samples of beer from each of the brewing plants across the country are flown in for this tasting. They all have to taste right and they have to taste the same. Someone on the tour asked, "What happens if they don't?" The guide said, "We send it to Miller." We all laughed at that.

Our son, Jim, is known as the beer connoisseur in our family. I was talking to our son, Mark, and told him where I was. He said, "Mom, you've been to a distillery and two breweries. Who are you taking this trip with, Jim the father or Jim the son?" Good question! It was fun, though. I've learned a lot. My mom would be so proud of me. Every night she had to have her one bottle of Bud before she went to bed. She loved her Bud! She would like that I visited a Budweiser brewery.

Tonight, we went to St. Charles for dinner and ate at an Irish Pub. No wonder Mark is wondering who I am with! St. Charles is an old historic town. It was the first capitol of Missouri. It is a beautiful town. The main street still has the old historic homes. Most of them have been turned into restaurants, shops, pubs, but all have retained their original historic value. The fact that they still exist today and are intact is probably due to the fact that they were all made of brick. We enjoyed strolling down this quaint street and soaking up the history of St. Charles.

Tomorrow, we will visit the old Cathedral in St. Louis, Daniel Boone's Homestead, and who knows what else. It will be fun. Jim has decided he also wants to see the largest fork. So now we have the largest ball of twine, the largest pencil, and the largest fork. Me – The Badlands, Crazy Horse, and Mt. Rushmore are calling my name.

Missouri **– The Show Me State**

State Motto – "Let the Welfare of the People be the Supreme Law"

License Plate Saying – Show Me State

Chapter 6

Before leaving St. Louis, we went to the Basilica/Cathedral of St. Louis IX. The Basilica dates back to 1907. We definitely wanted to see this Cathedral. We got there as the Angeles bells were ringing at 12:00 noon. Turns out there is Mass there every day at noon. We didn't know that; it was an added bonus. We stayed for mass and afterward toured the church.

The church is huge and it is exquisite; there are no other words for it. I thought my parish church in Philadelphia was the most beautiful church I had ever seen. Not next to this church! The whole church is done in mosaics – walls, ceiling, altars, etc. Each mosaic forms a happening in Jesus' life, a saint's life, happenings in the parish's history, history of the church, and a corresponding Bible verse surrounds the picture. To see these done as mosaics, with all the different colors blending and the gold sparkling from each one is magnificent. I did take lots of pictures, but I don't think pictures will do the church justice.

The outside of the church is equally as beautiful. There are four prayer gardens. The first one was The Angel of Peace. A large statue of an angel with two smaller angels stood in the middle of the garden. On the wings of the angels were chimes. A nice breeze was blowing and combined with the chimes, it made beautiful music. All along the path of the prayer gardens are bricks that were donated by many people. The bricks have their names engraved on them. Important people had their names engraved in gold. We saw a brick for Stan Musial (baseball) and his wife engraved in gold. While we were in one of the prayer gardens, the priest who said mass came out. We greeted him and talked for a few minutes. I hugged him goodbye and he said he would pray for our safe journey. Again, I cried, I felt so moved. A nun and now a priest are praying for us. Jim and I stood in one of the prayer gardens, held hands, and prayed ourselves. The whole experience was another beautiful, spiritual experience.

We do plan to see as many shrines, churches, and cathedrals as we can find in the cities we visit. One of our wishes is always for our safety on this trip. God is certainly answering that wish.

While we were in the Cathedral area, we drove around and looked at the neighborhood. It was very beautiful, with those old, very large, brick homes again. I'm sure that a lot of money lived there at one time. It was clearly evident that a lot of money lives there now. Everything was so well taken care of and the homes were beautiful.

From that area, we went to Forest Park. It is St. Louis' Central Park. It is unbelievable! It is 500 acres, bigger than Central Park in New York. The park contains a renowned zoo, which is free, a beautiful golf course, tennis courts, Art Museum, John F. Kennedy Memorial Forest, picnic grounds, lots of parking, hiking trails — anything and everything; you name it, this park has it. It is really beautiful. I've never seen a city park equal to Forest Park.

Sadly, we left St. Louis and got on our way to Springfield, MO. It started to rain as we left, so it was a good time to be in the car. I studied the clouds as we drove. They were so gray and so thick. It is easy to see why tornadoes hit this area so frequently and are so damaging.

You will be happy to know that Jim got one of his wishes today. Last night he told me that we missed the largest pencil, and that now he wanted to see the largest rocking chair instead. We took the highway most of the time, but we got off at one exit and went the backroads. Jim knew what he was doing. Sure enough, the largest rocking chair was on this road. It was on the infamous "Route 66." It was so cool. You wouldn't believe how big it was. I took Jim's picture in front of the rocking chair and he didn't even come up to the first cross bar on the bottom. It was constructed in 2008 and erected on April 1, 2008. It stands 42' 4" in height, it weighs 27,500 pounds, and is 20' across in width. It sits or towers right by an old country store that was a Route 66 popular spot to stop. It's funny, when we got off the highway and all the way here it was pouring. Just as we got to the largest rocking chair, the sun came out. We were able to get out of the car, see it, and take pictures. Jim was a happy man!!!

When we got back on the road, we saw signs for the largest candy store. Jim didn't know about that one. Of course, we had to stop. It was a very big candy store. There were barrels of candy. On one side of the store were barrels of the candy we knew as kids – Bonomo Turkish Taffy, B-B Bats, chicken puffs (coconut), watermelon candy slices, wax lips and fangs, wax soda bottles with flavored juice in them, etc. On the other side of the store were barrels of candy of today, along with 20 different flavors of salt water taffy and homemade fudge. There are bags all over the store for people to take and fill. Jim and I got bags and we happily filled our bags with all kinds of goodies. We literally were like two kids in a candy store! It was great fun. After we filled our bags, we took them to the counter to be weighed and we paid according to the weight. Guess whose bag weighed the most – right, Jim's. Again, he was a happy man!!!

We are now in Springfield, Missouri. Missouri is a big state. When you come to Missouri going to St. Louis, the ground is very flat. I can see why the pioneers chose St. Louis to cross the Missouri River on the barges. It was much easier to walk and drive their wagons on flat terrain. When we left St. Louis, we came to higher, hilly ground that would have been almost impossible to navigate with a wagon full of supplies, possessions, and no road. The hilly ground was lush with trees and it was beautifully green. We are looking forward to exploring Springfield tomorrow and continuing on to Branson.

Jim still wants to see the biggest fork and the biggest ball of twine. I think he will get his wish to see the biggest fork tomorrow. Me – the Corn Museum, The Badlands, Crazy Horse, and Mt. Rushmore are still calling my name.

Chapter 7

We started our day in Springfield, MO. Springfield is a city, but it is a small city. Other than the historic main street, there wasn't much to see. The University of Missouri and its campus take up most of downtown Springfield. The main street has the old buildings still intact, but the older homes were mostly fraternity and sorority houses. There must have been a shortage of bricks in Springfield because the big, old homes weren't made of brick and they weren't as nice as the other homes we saw. In fact, there were very few homes that were brick, contrary to the other homes we saw in Missouri. The biggest and nicest building I saw in Springfield was in a park-like setting. At first, I thought it was a park until we drove by and I read the sign. It was the U.S. Medical Center for Prisoners. It was completely made of brick and it was a beautiful facility. Imagine that – and it was for prisoners!!!

Springfield is the national headquarters for Bass Pro Shops. I had never been in a Bass Pro Shop. This store was almost 500,000 square feet. I stood there with my mouth open and my eyes open wider. I couldn't believe what I saw. The store was decorated like a forest inside with waterfalls, trees, ponds with fish, alligators, stuffed bears, deer, elk, mountain cats, fish tanks, along with all the sporting goods they sell. It was unbelievable. They should change their advertising slogan to "Come on down. Bring the kids. Stay for the day." And, you could do that; there were several restaurants in this store. There was even a museum about archery, hunting, fishing, and famous

24

people who have won Olympic gold medals, trophies and other medals in their sports, including President Teddy Roosevelt. He was quite a sportsman.

Jim has been to Cabela's and Bass Pro Shops. They have recently merged. This shop was awesome! Jim has taken our grandsons, Noah, Lucas, and Andrew to Cabela's when they come for their vacations with us. They go early in the morning and stay most of the day. Now I know why. Katie and Delaney (granddaughters) when you come for your vacation, we are going to Cabela's or a Bass Pro Shop for the day. These places are not just for boys; they are for girls, too.

One special thing we did see in Springfield that made Jim very happy – the largest fork. It was very large. It measured 35 feet in height. Jim only came up to the tines in the fork. Again, Jim knew exactly where it was. It was fun to see. Of course, we had our picture taken beside it.

Driving through Missouri on the interstates, the roads are good. The only congestion we hit was when we got to Branson. Branson is very crowded. I noticed as we drove through the state that there are walls of solid rock on either side of the road. They must have had to blast through the mountains/hills to make the roads. I was intrigued by the solid rock. I know they had to blast through the mountains to make the Northeast Extension of the PA Turnpike. Driving on the Northeast Extension, it's common to see rocks that have fallen laying on the ground. I didn't see anything like that on these roads. They are solid, straight up and down, walls of rock. Also, the roads are very clean. I didn't see trash thrown all over the roads, not even in the cities. Kentucky and Missouri are very clean states. That was nice to see.

Talk about glitz, that's Branson. It's a lot like Las Vegas, only in Las Vegas you get to see the real stars. The main road is one show after another, one hotel after another, one restaurant after another, and one souvenir store after another. However, once you get past the main road, Branson is very nice.

We are staying at our timeshare in Branson for the next few days. It's nice to have a little home away from home for a while. The timeshare sits high up on a hill and it is nice to look down at the town. It is a beautiful sight.

We are very close to Oklahoma here. I am hoping we can drive through some of Oklahoma, just so I can say I was there. I would like to see all of the state, but there isn't enough time in our schedule. That will have to be another trip.

Tonight, we drove to Table Rock Dam. It was built by the U.S. Army Corp of Engineers. They created this huge lake and park from the dam. It is outstanding. There is a beautiful hotel (chalet) that sits on top of the mountain looking down at the lake. It must be a great but expensive place to stay. Condos and home sites are offered for sale. The sun was setting when we were there and the sunset on the lake was exquisite. I had to stop and take a picture. It was very peaceful, beautiful, and quiet at this spot; a haven from the busyness of Branson. We are going on the Showboat Dinner Cruise tomorrow night and we'll get to see it again "up close and personal." Lucky us!

Along with the largest fork, we also saw the largest chicken sculpture on the main road in Branson. Who would have thought; the largest rocking chair, the largest fork, the largest chicken sculpture – maybe there is something to Jim's desire to see all these things. Tomorrow we are going to see the largest toy museum. I bet he finds his childhood toy soldiers and toy gun and holster there.

For Jim – the largest ball of twine is coming up! Me – I'm happy seeing everything, but Kansas City, the Corn Museum, The Badlands, Crazy Horse, and Mt. Rushmore are waiting!

P.S. Guess whose bag of candy is gone already? Nope, not mine!

Chapter 8

We just came from the Showboat Dinner Cruise in Branson. It was fantastic. We didn't know what to expect and were pleasantly surprised. The boat was beautiful, inside and out. It looked just like the Cotton Blossom in the movie "Showboat." It was a real paddle wheel boat, all white, with the name "Branson Belle." It sailed on Table Rock Lake that surrounds Branson. It was great; so smooth, we didn't even know we were moving.

I don't know how this happened, but we were in the front row for the show and had amazing seats. We started off with dinner, which was very good. During dinner, the performers did some entertaining, but the real show came after dinner. It was called, "Made for America." There was a Master of Ceremonies who also was a magician, a male singing group called, "The Showmen," a female vocalist who was also an acrobat, played the violin and piano, and a performing band. Each were great. The show was wonderful. The talent that was on that stage was amazing. We didn't realize the quality of performers in Branson. The theme of the show was a Tribute to America. There were songs about America, songs made famous in America, Motown music, Big Band music; you name it, they did it – all to rousing applause.

The magician was great. He got a little boy from the audience to help him. The little boy was so cute. He laughed through his whole skit. I couldn't help laughing along with him. The magician's tricks were amazing. They were not your run-of-the-mill magic tricks, but really good ones. He got a woman to come up on the stage with him when he did his Houdini routine. We all watched as she buckled him tightly in the strait jacket, and we all watched as he got out of the strait jacket. It was unbelievable! I am not big on magic tricks, but I loved this show.

The woman performer was wonderful. When she first came on stage, she played the violin. The next time she came out, she played the piano. For her third performance, she sang, "I Believe I Can Fly" and began doing a flying acrobatic routine while playing the violin. She was amazing! We couldn't believe how talented she was. She was a graduate of Julliard in New York, served in the Navy, and has performed on many cruise ships.

The Showmen were fantastic. The songs they sang and the routines they did were wonderful. They sang a lot of Motown songs. The dances and moves they did for each song made us want to get up and dance right along with them. Their voices were awesome. Each time they performed, whether it was gospel, rock, or Americana, they were great.

The band was very good. They played songs by themselves and also with the other performers. In the beginning of their part of the show, they played Glenn Miller songs. All I could think of was my deceased brother-in-law, Bill (Dutch) who loved Glenn Miller. He would have enjoyed the band so much. They played every kind of music and were great musicians.

At the end of the show, all the acts came together for a Tribute to America medley. There was a screen in back of them, and pictures of America came on the screen during the performance. That was awesome and had all of us standing on our feet clapping. It was a wonderful, feel-good show. Jim and I made a great choice in what we picked to see in Branson. I asked Jim, "Which one of our grandchildren would have loved being here?" He said, "All of them." That's exactly what I was thinking. I wished they were there with us. Branson definitely is a family resort.

We didn't get to the Largest Toy Museum today. We wanted

to see the old town of Branson. Branson is very beautiful. It is surrounded by the Ozark Mountains and Lake Taneycomo. The old town is very nice, quaint and quiet — unlike the show part of the city. They have a special part of the city called The Landings. It is built along Lake Taneycomo. There are very high-end stores on the ground level, along with many restaurants. Condos were built over the stores, looking out over the lake. There were many fountains and dancing waters throughout The Landings. We spent the afternoon walking along the river, looking in the shops, and just enjoying being there.

We didn't get to see Daniel Boone's Homestead. It was too far from where we were traveling. I am sure there will be other places we won't get to, also, but it doesn't matter. We are loving everything we are seeing. This is supposed to be an easy trip and we aren't going to rush to fit things in or get anywhere. We will see what we see.

Tomorrow, I am hoping to see the John Denver Tribute before we leave Branson. How could I ever leave without seeing that?! It is at 10:00 am. I don't get up early, but I will to see a John Denver tribute.

So — Jim didn't get to see the toy museum and he didn't find his toy soldiers or toy gun and holster, but the largest ball of twine still awaits him. At first, I thought he was joking about these things. I didn't think they were real, but they are. Who knew?! And, they really were fun to see, especially to see Jim so happy seeing them. Me — it's still on to our granddaughter, Ashley, Kansas City, The Corn Museum, The Badlands, Crazy Horse, and Mt. Rushmore. Can't wait!

Chapter 9

Yes, Maggie, we are in Kansas!

I didn't get to see the John Denver Tribute today in Branson. Jim wanted to show me Big Brutus. No, not what you are thinking!!! Big Brutus is the second largest electric power shovel in the world. More about Big Brutus later.

We decided to go to Wichita instead of Kansas City because Cowtown is there where reenactments of the Old West are held. Growing up like we did on cowboy and Indian movies and TV shows, we wanted to see that. It's supposed to be a replica of an old cowboy town. It should be fun.

We got an early start and drove part of the way on historic Route 66. Compared to the super highways of today, Route 66 seems like an old country road. We passed mile after mile of farms. The farm houses were unique. They were built completely of stone. Some were made of small stones, some medium stones, and some large stones. They were beautiful little homes and looked comfy. I'm sure most of them have been there for 100 years or more and people used what was plentiful then to build their homes, like bricks in Missouri.

Kansas is beautiful. We are now in Wichita and settled in for the night. It is good to be off the road. We had fun, though. We had our own John Denver show while driving. I played one of his CD's and we sang along. One of the songs he sings is "Matthew." It is about his uncle who grew up in Kansas. One of the lines goes, "Blue as the

Kansas summer sky." When we heard that, we looked up and, sure enough, the Kansas sky was very blue and it was beautiful.

We haven't seen much of Wichita. We will explore tomorrow, but from what I have seen, it is a pretty affluent city. Kansas is quite a contrast to Missouri. Kansas is very flat. For as far as I could see, the land was flat; there were no mountains in the distance. I saw rows and rows of corn, many wheat bundles, and cattle all over. I don't know if today is an exception or the norm, but it is also very windy. I'll find out more tomorrow.

We did get to see Big Brutus. Jim really took me by surprise with this. What can I tell you about Big Brutus?! It is SO large. It is huge. I took a picture of Jim standing by it and he didn't even come up to the tire tread on it. Big Brutus is a power shovel and it was used in strip mining coal in Kansas in the 1960's to 1990's. I didn't know they had coal mining in Kansas, but in the late 1880's, the state supplied coal to the railroads. Big Brutus was an engineering marvel for its time because it was electric and could pick up enough coal in one lift to fill three railroad cars. Big Brutus is 16 stories tall and weighs 11 million pounds. There was also a museum on the site. I enjoyed seeing that, too, and the mining equipment used in this area.

As I mentioned before, my grandfather was a coal miner in upstate PA. In going to see Big Brutus and the museum, I learned that coal mining in Kansas, Colorado, etc. was very different from coal mining in the East. My grandfather mined anthracite coal. To do that, geologists would find where there was coal and miners would dig into the ground to find the coal vein. Once they found it, they dug deep into the mine. The miners made rope elevator shafts to go up and down from the mine and into different levels of the mine. Once they extracted all the coal from one vein, they would go onto another spot and find the vein there. In Kansas, the men mined bituminous coal. Again, geologists would find the coal close to the surface and Big Brutus would dig 110 tons in one scoop, creating a huge trench and extract the coal. No matter what the method, coal mining was very hard and very dangerous work. Big Brutus made the work a little better for the miners in the mid-west.

According to family stories, the miners in the mid-west/west were paid better than miners in the east. My mom's brother, my Uncle John Fisher, left PA when he was in his 20's to go to the west to mine coal because he thought he could make more money there. He went to Colorado. Unfortunately, he got pneumonia early on and died in a hospital there. My grandparents were heartbroken. I still have the telegram the hospital sent telling them of his death. John was used to cold and stormy weather in PA, but he wasn't a match for the Colorado winters.

I listened to my grandfather's mining tales from the time I was a little girl. They are a part of me and will be with me always. However, I really didn't know what the life of a coal miner was truly like until I went on a tour of the No. 9 Lansford Coal Mine in Lansford, PA, outside of Jim Thorpe. Our group was taken deep into the coal mine. The mine is cold, wet, and dark. The temperature is in the mid-50 degrees in the mine every day of the year. The men started their day at 6:00 am and didn't finish until 6:00 pm. In the winter, they never saw daylight. My grandfather began working in the mines when he was eight years old as a breaker boy. Male children had to go to work as soon as they could to help the family. Breaker boys sat at the top of the coal chutes. The coal ran very fast down the chutes. As the coal was coming down the chute, the boys separated the good coal from the rock coal with their hands and feet, often losing toes, feet, and fingers in the process. And, they did this for the grand sum of 10 cents a day.

My grandfather went on to be a coal miner and spent 48 years of his life in this dangerous profession. Once he was trapped in a cave-in. The area in the mine where my grandfather was working caved in and he was trapped. The only way to get him out was to dynamite the area but they didn't know exactly where he was. One of the miners put a pipe in the ground and called into the pipe, "Hello, Jimmy. Where are you?" He did this at various spots in the ground until my grandfather called back at one spot, "I'm down here." The miner told him to measure 12' back and stay there. Miners measured feet by the boots they wore. The boots were 12 inches, so using their boots and taking 12 steps back would bring my grandfather to a safe place where the dynamite wouldn't hurt him. While my grandmother and great-grandmother knelt and prayed at home, the miner dynamited the area. It was midnight before the other miners reached my grandfather, but he was brought out safely. My grandparents had 12 children, six boys and six girls. When my grandfather, covered in coal dust, walked down the street after being rescued, his children ran to him, climbing all over him, crying, "Daddy, Daddy." They were overjoyed that their daddy was alive. I pictured this scene so vividly in my mind's eye. When my mom would tell this part of the story, it never failed to bring tears to my eyes. Still does!

Mining was and still is a dangerous profession. It has come a long way from my grandfather's time. Back in the days of my grandfather, it was nothing short of slave labor. Thankfully, there have been improvements in safety, benefits, and salary. So, seeing Big Brutus today was reconnecting me, again, with my roots. Thanks, Jim!

Well, the largest ball of twine still awaits – and whatever else Jim can find for us to see. I know the Ford Museum in Dearborn, MI is on his agenda. Let's see, Jim has seen the World's Largest Rocking Chair, World's Largest Fork, World's Largest Candy Store, and now the World's Largest Power Shovel. Me – I'm still waiting – Cowtown, Ashley, The Corn Palace, The Badlands, Crazy Horse, and Mt. Rushmore, I am on my way!

Chapter 10

In that same song, "Matthew," John Denver also writes, "Gold is just a windy Kansas wheat field …" Now I know what he meant. Kansas is WINDY, very windy. The wind doesn't stop. I asked a few people we met who live in Kansas about the wind. One man said, "What wind?" He was oblivious to it and told me you get used to it when you live there. It was 91 degrees in Wichita today and all the people said they were glad for the wind or it would be so hot.

We started the day off by visiting the Cathedral of the Immaculate Conception. We couldn't believe we were in another church named Immaculate Conception. There was a service going on when we entered. We thought it was a wedding but the girl/woman was dressed in aqua. The boys/men were dressed in matching shirts, black pants, and a black hat. The service was in Spanish, so we didn't know what was being said. After the service, I asked a woman if that was a wedding. She explained to me that it was a Mexican Quinceanera. When a girl turns 15, her family has a ceremony to welcome her into womanhood. The girl gets dressed very fancy, there is a church ceremony, and then a party afterward. She looked beautiful. You never know what you are going to learn.

The Cathedral was beautiful. The paintings around the church were exquisite, especially the one of the dove around the huge holy water fountain. We got pictures of the church and made our three wishes. Your intentions were lifted up in our wishes. One thing we have found in our travels is that there are a lot of churches in the mid-west – churches of every denomination, and they are big churches. We didn't have to look far or travel far without seeing a church. America is still very much a Christian country.

From the Cathedral, we went to the Old Cowtown Museum. Cowtown is a replica of the way the town of Wichita looked back in the 1870's. They moved existing buildings to this site along the Arkansas River and refurbished them. The city of Wichita spent $13,000 for ten miles of wooden sidewalks when the city was growing. The boards were still prevalent when we went to Cowtown.

Cowtown was made up of a few one-room log cabins, several homes of the well-to-do, a church, a one-room school house, general store, meat market, blacksmith shop, dressmaker, saddle shop, saloon, train station, dance hall, newspaper, horses, wagons, stagecoach, gunslingers, and a farm. It was a working town, with people dressed in periodic garb doing their various jobs. The people in the shops explained to us what they were doing. It was very interesting and, of course, I had to check everything out. I had a "Sarsaparilla" in the saloon. It was really good; tasted just like root beer.

In the dance hall, we watched very well-dressed men and women doing dances from that era. After they demonstrated the waltz in various steps and tempos, they asked the visitors to dance with them. Of course, Jim was asked to dance. He did one of the faster waltzes with his partner and he did great. In that day, people switched partners during the dance so they could get to know each other. Jim's next partner was a little girl around five. She was adorable and he was so great dancing with her. The little girl was thrilled! When we first went into the dance hall, Jim said to me, emphatically, "I am not dancing!" He changed his mind when asked; he did great; and he had a good time. That didn't surprise me. Jim is a good dancer and he always has fun.

The homes of the well-to-do were beautiful. We were surprised at how elegantly they were furnished and how large they were. The furniture was shipped in from very well-known furniture stores in the East. There was a front parlor that was used only for guests. It contained all of their valuable furnishings and decorations. Across from that was the dining room, followed by a kitchen and family parlor. Upstairs there were two bedrooms. For that day and time, the homes were outstanding.

The cabins were small, but well built, proved by their existence to this day. One was a two-room cabin with a bedroom in the back. The cabin was owned and built by an African American. The husband died very young and left the woman with two young children. She used the back bedroom as a hotel room for visitors to help support her and her children. She later ran a hotel in the town. Still, she lived in the log cabin house until she was quite old. Her children donated it to Cowtown after she passed away.

We saw a gunfight, sat with the cowboys in the saloon, talked to the dressmaker, blacksmith, and anyone else we could find to talk to and answer our questions. The gunfight was realistically staged and fun to watch. I wouldn't have wanted to be around for a real one though. I was surprised by the portraits of scantily-clad women in the saloon. The pictures were very old. They appeared to be pictures, but were more like paintings or portraits. Perhaps they were of the saloon girls and were there for their patrons, the cowboys. After weeks or months on the trail, the cowboys had to have something to look at other than cows!

The dressmaker had an old Singer sewing machine. Women made their everyday dresses or bought them for $2.00. Fancy dresses were made by the dressmaker. They were about $20.00. I don't imagine women had many fancy dresses back then at that price. The fancy dresses the women wore at the dance hall were beautiful. They were decorated with lace, embroidery, braiding, ribbons, etc. I was surprised that they were so pretty.

Many people came to Wichita from Philadelphia, Boston, New York, and cities and towns all along the East Coast. They came at a great time when Wichita was beginning to bloom. They gave their knowledge and talent and helped make Wichita a boom town. The people began banks, schools, businesses, railroads, and became very wealthy in the process. When cattle began being sent to Dodge City instead of Wichita because of quarantine laws, the city continued to prosper because they were so well entrenched in the grain, flour, and railroad businesses. Many of the people came as immigrants through Ellis Island. They heard of the coal industry in Kansas. They were hard workers and became miners or small business owners. The Germans were very prosperous in the mid-west.

The dance hall in the town was started by the Germans so people could get to know each other and have enjoyable times. We had a great time at Cowtown and learned a lot, even the waltz. Men may have built the mid-west, but thank God, the women civilized it.

I don't know how the early settlers stood the howling prairie wind. When we left Wichita, we drove through more of Kansas to Nebraska. Along the way, there were very few towns. We saw very large farms, waving wheat, a lot of cattle, and prairie for miles and miles. The people of that time must have rarely seen their neighbors, they were all so far apart. Being alone on the prairie, living in a log cabin or sod house, must have been very lonely. The incessant wind added to that loneliness, I am sure. Along the way, there were fences on the farms where cattle were lined up in rows against the fence. We think they were lined up that way to avoid the wind. Kansas and Nebraska are so windy because there are no mountains and few trees. The wind just whips right through with nothing to stop it.

While we were driving to Nebraska, we had dark clouds with us. We seemed to be just on the edge of the clouds all the way. Cars and trucks were passing us with a lot of electronic equipment on them. There were also a lot of cars and trucks parked on the side of the road. They all were storm chasers, chasing the storm that eluded us, and watching for tornadoes. We couldn't believe how many people chased storms. We are very glad to be off the road tonight!

Well, Jim finally found the Holy Grail. He found the largest ball of twine. It was in a little town in Kansas, Cawker City, about 40 miles from the Nebraska border. It was cool and it really does exist. The largest ball of twine sits inside this large outdoor building and weighs about 20,000 pounds. We were walking all around it, touching it, and taking pictures when a car pulled up and a family got out. They were from Oklahoma, saw us taking pictures, and wanted to see what we were doing. We told them about the largest ball of twine, we all laughed, and then took pictures of each other by the largest ball of twine. Jim was a happy man today. Only Jim!!!

Jim is now looking forward to seeing Ashley, Chicago, and the Ford Museum. Me – Ashley, Chicago, The Corn Palace, The Badlands, Crazy Horse, and Mt. Rushmore are within reach. We'll be in South Dakota tomorrow. My turn!

Kansas   The Sunflower State
State Motto – "To the Stars Through Difficulties"
License Plate Saying – Wheat State

Chapter 11

Talk about wide open spaces – you have no idea what wide open spaces are until you have traveled the mid-west. Under blue skies, sunshine, and puffy white clouds, we had a front row seat to the most incredible panorama of beauty. Trees, grass in different shades of green, cows, horses, immaculate farms, flat plains, and rolling hills – all were ours to enjoy, and enjoy we did!

Nebraska is beautiful. It is flat as far as you can see, but the plains have their own beauty. We were on a major road, but the towns were very few and far between. When we did come upon a town, it was a one-street town. It was a quiet, peaceful ride, with plenty of time to observe, and no stress to hurry from other cars. The grass on one side of the road was a different shade of green than the other side. It reminded me of Ireland and all the different shades of green there. There were many fences on the side of the road, but cows and horses roamed freely inside. There were so many cows, mostly Black Angus, and the world was theirs, with so much ground on which to roam. Wheat fields, cornfields, small watering ponds, big watering ponds, flowers growing wild in fields, all of nature's beauty laid out just for us. To all of the above, add towering hills surrounding everything, and you have incredible beauty.

In Nebraska, we were riding parallel to railroad tracks. Along the tracks we saw at least 20 different trains, each carrying 130 hopper cars of coal. They weren't moving, just sitting there. Yes, we did count. We were amazed to see so many trains. It was nice to see that a lot of trains are still being utilized. The trains were the BNSF (Burlington Northern-Santa Fe) coming from the Powder River Basin in Wyoming and Montana, the largest coal producing area in the United States. They were probably heading toward Grand Island, Nebraska. What was so amazing is that each train had three engines. They were just parked there -- at least 90 engines. I guess Warren Buffet knows something we don't. His company owns the BNSF! The trains were probably backup coal for mid-west electric generation plants. We thought they weren't running because it was Sunday. We stopped at a country gas station and asked about them. We were told that they were going east towards Grand Island and that a lot of things don't run on Sundays.

South Dakota is even more beautiful than Nebraska. We arrived at The Badlands this afternoon and spent several hours there. The Badlands is a National Park. For $10, senior citizens get a lifetime pass – not bad. The Park covers only 20 miles of Badlands that you can visit. The Badlands go on for many more miles. I have to admit, I really didn't know what The Badlands were. I thought they were where a battle took place or a very wild western town. The Badlands are incredible formations of clay and sand, rising up from the ground, and towering above everything. They were named The Badlands by French explorers because there wasn't enough water there to sustain human life. When the oceans receded the formations rose, and they have existed for thousands of years.

After stopping at the Visitors' Center, we drove through The Badlands. There are different stops along the road to get out of the car, view them, take pictures, etc. When we stopped, I couldn't believe that people were climbing all over the formations. The surface of the formation crumbled in my hand. I was surprised, but later found out that the surface was popcorn soil for that reason. The interior of the formation is solid and does not crumble.

When we got out of the car, I also couldn't believe how wonderful the air smelled. When we were in the Visitors' Center, I asked what was that wonderful smell. I was told it was sweet clover. It was wonderful. Everything smelled so good, I wished that I could bottle up the aroma and take it home.

The Visitors' Center begins with a movie about The Badlands. There was also a museum about the area. The Badlands are home to many varieties of animals. Bears used to live there, but because of the lack of water, they are gone. The movie, the museum, and the viewing places to stop along the way are great.

At the Visitors' Center, I learned that the Lakota Indians went to The Badlands to avoid U.S. soldiers. Many perished there, also from the lack of water. There have been and still are many excavations in the formations and the land that have revealed enough fossil bones to supply science centers and museums throughout the country. Prairie dogs, ferrets, snakes, deer, big horned sheep, wolves, and other animals call The Badlands home. We saw a whole colony of prairie dogs poking up from their holes. Two bighorn sheep crossed the road in front of our car, and two others were on the other side. The Badlands are awesome, very interesting, and a must see to really appreciate them.

While we were riding, there were signs all along the road for the Wall Drug Store. The signs advertised free ice water, five-cent coffee, T-Rex, ice cream, etc., so we decided to stop and see what it was all about. The store was in the town of Wall. The store took up a whole town block. It had everything you could possibly want. It also had a restaurant. We were hungry by this time so we ate there. It was very good and reasonable.

Ted Hauster graduated from pharmacy school back in the 30's. He wanted to open a drug store in a small town that had a Catholic Church. He and his wife found Wall, South Dakota and set up shop. They were from the East, but decided to settle in Wall. The drug store wasn't doing well. Ted's wife suggested that he advertise on the main highway, "Free Ice Water." People were thirsty, they came, and the drug store grew into this booming business/store that has everything. It is a drug store, clothing store, ice cream store, fudge shop, sporting goods store, souvenir store, restaurant, and each room has something different, along with art and historic pictures. Outside, in the back of the store is a playground for children. It was amazing, and all from free ice water. The word "FREE" is always a good sell! The store also had a "Travelers' Chapel." I made sure I stopped there. It was a beautiful little chapel. Where else would you find something like that except small town America!

I am finally in South Dakota, staying at a hotel just outside Mt. Rushmore. Tomorrow, I will see Mt. Rushmore and Crazy Horse. Jim saw something he didn't know about today – the largest drug store. He was very impressed and he was a happy man. Jim has added Notre Dame to his list, along with Ashley, Chicago, and the Ford Museum. Me – Mt. Rushmore and Crazy Horse are at my beck and call. Lots of exciting things to see tomorrow!

P.S. You will be happy to know that Maggie hasn't made a squeak.

Nebraska **The Cornhusker State**
State Motto – "Equality Before the Law"
License Plate Saying – Cornhusker State

Chapter 12

We just came from the evening ceremony at Mt. Rushmore. It was AMAZING! I see patriotism being chipped at and eroding on the East and West Coasts, but not here in the heart of the country.

There wasn't a seat left in the amphitheater. It was standing room only. A speaker came on stage and spoke about the four Presidents who were honored on Mt. Rushmore. Next, a movie was shown about the monument and those Presidents' lives. A spotlight began to shine on Mt. Rushmore while "America The Beautiful" was sung and scenes from America were shown on the screen. We were then asked to stand and sing the National Anthem. As tears formed, Jim and I held hands and sang with everyone else. Afterward men and women who had served in the different branches of our military were asked to come on stage. Each were introduced, their branch of the military mentioned, and they were honored with much applause from the people attending. The flag was lowered and the ceremony concluded. The entire ceremony was reverent, respectful, and so moving. Because of the bad storms today, we didn't think the ceremony would be held tonight. However, the storm stopped around seven; the sun came out; and we left to be here. We are so glad we didn't miss this ceremony. It was truly an honor to be here!

This afternoon we went to Mt. Rushmore. How can I describe Mt. Rushmore?! Mere words will not do it justice. It is magnificent, majestic, inspiring, awesome, moving, beautiful – all that and more.

There is a museum at the base of the monument. The museum

itself was amazing to see. In the museum, I learned that the monument took 14 years to complete. It was designed by Gutzon Borglum, supervised by him, worked on by him personally, and built with the help of miners and workmen from the town of Keystone. Keystone is high up in the mountains and once was a booming gold mining town. I learned why Washington, Jefferson, Lincoln, and Theodore Roosevelt were chosen to be honored on the Mt. Rushmore monument. Washington was chosen because he led our country through the Revolutionary War and our country's beginnings. Jefferson was chosen because of his writing of the Declaration of Independence and his foresight in making the Louisiana Purchase and extending our boundaries. Lincoln was chosen because he, too, led our country through another dark time, and because he believed that "All men are created equal," and because he would not dissolve the Union over this issue. Theodore Roosevelt was chosen because he was a fearless leader and because of his wisdom in creating National Parks to preserve our land for future generations.

Inside the museum was a bookstore and the only remaining worker was signing copies of the book he wrote about the construction of the monument. Jim and I met him, talked to him, and, of course, bought his book, "Mount Rushmore Questions and Answers." His name was Don "Nick" Clifford. He grew up in Keystone, South Dakota and was a driller in the gold mines. He was very nice, very easy to talk to, and very interesting. I asked him if he knew at the time that he was working on something that would be so monumental to our country. He told me that he didn't know. He said that he was just doing a job and was happy to have the job. He got the job because he was a good baseball pitcher. Sculptor, Gutzon Borglum, wanted to field a good team. Nick was the youngest on the project. He started at $.55 an hour. Later, as a driller he made $1.65 an hour. A regular workman made $.65 an hour. They were considered good wages for the 1930's. It was an honor meeting him and talking to him. I got a picture of him and Jim together.

Mt. Rushmore sits high atop South Dakota's Black Hills. We

could see it long before we got to the top. It commands the mountain and your attention. Mt. Rushmore stands 60' high. Looking at it, I could not help but be inspired and so proud to be a part of the history of this great country.

From Mt. Rushmore, we went to the monument being carved of Chief Crazy Horse. What was completed was outstanding; however, in 50 years, only his face has been finished. The Chief Crazy Horse monument will be twice the size of Mt. Rushmore – quite a huge project.

The sculptor of Chief Crazy Horse was Korczak Ziolkowski. He designed it and worked on it himself for 15 years because he did not want government help and especially not government intervention. He died in 1982 and his family has respected his wish. Seven of his ten children presently work on the project. I understand Korczak's wish and his family respecting it, but I would think that in 50 years, they would have hired workers to help complete the monument. Hired workers would not be the government. The entrance to the Chief Crazy Horse monument is free, but between the parking fee, the gift shop, the museum, and the restaurant, they must take in quite a lot in one day, certainly enough to hire people to speed up the project.

Korczak Ziolkowski was from Massachusetts. He was commissioned by Henry Standing Bear (an elder in the Lakota tribe) to make this monument to Crazy Horse to honor all that the American Indians did for this country, their accomplishments, and subsequent losses. Chief Crazy Horse refused to sign a treaty and refused to be put on a reservation. He led a war party at the battle of Little Big Horn (Custer's Last Stand). Chief Crazy Horse was stabbed in the back and killed by one of the soldiers at Ft. Robinson in Crawford, Nebraska. He was known as a very brave warrior.

My heart has always gone out to the American Indians. They lived well on this land, respected it, and did not waste anything. We were ruthless in dealing with them. We came and we took, and we believed rightly so. It was not right. When I retired, I always thought I would be working among the American Indians. I wanted to help them in some way. I was going to work on a reservation in some capacity. My sympathy for them went that deep. It's what I had planned to do, but God had other plans for me.

Before the coming of the white man, there were 70 million bison/buffalo that roamed the prairies and the west. The buffalo sustained the American Indians and were very important in helping them to live. Every part of the buffalo was used by them to exist in their daily lives. After the white men came and killed the buffalos for sport and for furs, there were only around 1,000 left. Buffalo were almost extinct. This greatly hurt the American Indians and their livelihood. This and being put on reservations began the decline of the American Indian. Now, thanks to planning and preserves for buffalos, they have increased in numbers, but they will never be as numerous as they once were, nor will American Indians lives ever be the same. Very sad!

I LOVED being at this monument today. The museum was wonderful. There were many exhibits, artifacts, and guides to answer questions or inform us of certain rituals and historic facts. I could have spent all day just in the museum, learning and drenching myself in American Indian lore.

Yesterday, I said to Jim, "I would love to meet an American Indian and speak with him/her face to face." Today, I did that. One of the things they had outside the museum was a free show of American Indians demonstrating their dances. They were in an outside theater with seats. By the time I got there, the seats were taken. I stood in the back; someone left and I sat in the back. Another person left and I moved up. Someone in the second row left and I moved up. Then, someone in the first row left and I was front and center. It was wonderful. I had a front row seat!

The native men doing the dances were a grandfather (51), his son (19), and his grandson (17). They were so good, I closed my eyes and imagined I was in their camp, sitting around the campfire and being a part of this ritual. I could not take my eyes off them, their movements, and facial expressions. They did eight different American Indian dances, each more wonderful than the other. Some of the movements I could interpret. I believe that when the son held the eagle feather, kissed it, and waved it upward, he was giving thanks to the Great Spirit. I was in awe watching them.

The American Indian dancers were in full Native Indian regalia. Their regalia was beautifully adorned with beads, feathers, etc. The grandfather's outfit weighed 90 pounds. His head piece was authentic with eagle feathers and the actual head of an eagle was right in the middle of the back of the headpiece. I never saw that before. They and their dances were quite a sight to see.

Before they began their dance, the grandfather spoke to the crowd. He was very gentle, very wise, and very learned. He did not speak with bitterness. He told us that his ancestors, the Lakota's were forced from their reservation and made to walk the "Trail of Tears." When they got there, instead of being relocated, they were shot and buried alive. He said, "Isn't it ironic that so many years later, the largest supply of oil in the world has been found on an Indian reservation in the Dakotas." To me, it is not just ironic, it is rightly so. Justice! I hope the American Indians of today have learned from their ancestors and deal with the government shrewdly in this matter. Every treaty our ancestors made with them was broken. I hope that we have learned from our mistakes, too. The grandfather told us that Johnny Depp bought the ground where those American Indians were buried in a mass grave and gave it to them. It now belongs to the Lakota Indians.

I did get to talk to the grandfather. I told him how much I enjoyed watching the dances. Jim and I talked to him for a few minutes, got our picture taken with him, his son and grandson, and then went on to look at the monument more closely. This close-up experience with the American Indian dancers was one of the highlights of my day.

Tomorrow, we leave Rapid City and begin our move back East. We will visit The Corn Palace. I am looking forward to that. Jim, not so much. He has his sights set on Notre Dame, the Ford Museum, and Chicago. Me – I have Ashley, Chicago, and The Rock and Roll Hall of Fame. It's going to be great!

P.S. During the torrential rain, hail, thunder, and lightning storm today, the electricity went out in the hotel. I was going to the car when it happened and I got trapped in the elevator. Jim was in the room. It wasn't fun, but I didn't panic. I pushed the Emergency Button and got help. Now I know how bad the storms are in this part of the country. They are BAD! God is SO with us.

South Dakota   **The Mount Rushmore State**
State Motto – "Under God the People Rule"
License Plate Saying – Great Faces State

Chapter 13

We left Rapid City, South Dakota this morning and are now in Sioux Falls, South Dakota. We spent a lot of time driving, but managed to see a few things. We toured Rapid City before we left. It is a beautiful town. The historic part has been preserved. On the corners of the streets were statues of prominent people who helped build the town. The statues were also of cows, buffalo, American Indians, children, etc. It was cool seeing all the bronze statues. Each corner had something different. Rapid City was once a one-street town, but has grown and is continuing to grow. Many new homes, stores, and buildings have sprung up on the outskirts. I predict that one day it will be a budding metropolis with all the tourism from Mt. Rushmore and people moving there to live. Also, outside of Rapid City is Ellsworth Air Force Base, home of the Global Strike Command, B-1 bombers.

On the way to Sioux Falls, we stopped in Mitchell, South Dakota. Jim found another world's largest that we both wanted to see – The Corn Palace. It was fun to see. With its beautiful domes, it reminded me of a palace. There are large murals all over the front of the palace and the murals are all made of corn. Each year there is a different theme. This year's theme is "Remember When." The murals were of a farmer driving a tractor, horse-drawn carts, early telephones, and a soda fountain, to name a few. They were completely made of corn. There are seven varieties of corn that are different colors. The colored corn is used to make the murals, along with regular corn. The guide said, "Think of it as a paint-by-number, only with corn." It was incredible to see these beautiful murals completely made of corn.

The Corn Palace dates back to 1892. Mitchell was vying for capitol of South Dakota with the city of Pierre. They wanted to come up with something that would aid their cause and enrich their city financially. Two men came up with The Corn Palace. Aberdeen had the Grain Palace, Rapid City had the Alfalfa Palace, but no one had a Corn Palace. The others are gone, but the World's Largest Corn Palace still stands in Mitchell, South Dakota. It is SO worth seeing.

Inside, the Palace is used for basketball games, proms, civic events, shows, and galas. There is also a museum that tells about The Corn Palace through the years, how it got started, and many corn murals, including one of Mt. Rushmore. They were beautiful. There was a store that featured many things made of corn, including candy. I got my grandchildren corn lollipops. They are supposed to taste like buttered corn. I wonder how they will like them.

The townspeople decided to have a celebration in August when The Corn Palace first opened. John Philip Sousa and his band were invited to the first celebration. It was such a success that they now have a celebration annually in August to celebrate their plentiful bounty of corn. This has been going on for 122 years. They must be doing something right.

There are very bad storms right now and a tornado warning here and in Nebraska. I am going to get off the computer while I still have service. I am also going to stay in our room and not get trapped in another elevator.

Tomorrow, we are on to Minneapolis. We are going to see the Mall of America, the biggest mall in America. Does Jim have a preoccupation with seeing the largest of everything?! The Spam Museum, Notre Dame, and the Ford Museum still await Jim. Me – now that I've seen some of my favorites, I am eagerly looking forward to Ashley, Chicago, Amana Colony in Iowa, and The Rock and Roll Hall of Fame. Stay tuned!

Picture of author

Jim and I with Clydesdale Horse at Budweiser Brewery

Jim in front of the World's Largest Rocking Chair

Jim in front of Big Brutus

The Largest Ball of Twine

Mt. Rushmore

53

*Native American Indian dancers. Crazy
Horse Monument in the background.*

The Corn Palace

World's Largest Fork

Actual chair President Lincoln was sitting in at Ford Theater when he was assassinated. Blood stains still clearly visible.

World's Largest Hot Dog

Chapter 14

Today, we are back in civilization, and I'm not so sure we want to be – a big city and a mall in one day – too much. We liked the wide-open spaces! We are in Bloomington, outside of Minneapolis.

Last night was pretty scary, I have to admit. I didn't like being in a tornado area. I went to the lobby of the hotel and people were huddled around the TV, following the storm. We even had an official storm tracker in our midst. Thank God, we had nothing more than bad thunderstorms in Sioux Falls. However, I did read today that a tornado touched down north of Mitchell, South Dakota where we were yesterday. I am so glad we missed it!

Before leaving Sioux Falls, we went to see the battleship U.S. South Dakota Memorial. We were very pleasantly surprised. The town did a wonderful job with the memorial. The U. S. South Dakota was the most decorated battleship in World War II. It was built in Camden, New Jersey. Usually battleships have 15 to 30 years of service, but this ship was retired five years after it was built because it had seen so much service. It was involved in many battles during the war. The U.S. South Dakota was retired to the Navy Yard in Philadelphia, PA. Camden and Philadelphia were very much a part of our lives. We were surprised to read of their connection to the battleship.

The Memorial is located in the downtown area of Sioux Falls. It is in a field the whole length and width of the original ship. The front of the ship is outlined by wood at one end of the field, wood coming down the field for the middle of the ship, and the back of the ship is outlined in wood at the other end. In the middle of the field is what would have been the middle of the ship. Along the outside walls of the middle are plaques honoring the U.S. South Dakota for all the battles it was in. Plaques are located all around the outside, also, telling more of the story of this great ship.

Inside the circular middle is a museum, a movie telling the history of the ship, and videos of some of the men who served on the ship speaking about their time on it during the war. The people of South Dakota wanted to bring the ship home, but that wasn't possible. It was too badly damaged. The ship was broken up and sold for scrap. However, the Navy managed to salvage one of the guns, the propeller, engine, and many other parts of the ship, including the wood from the decks. They are on display inside and outside of the museum. The wood from the decks was teak. They were able to salvage so much of the wood that it adorns the whole interior of the museum. The ceiling and the walls of the museum are the decking from the U. S. South Dakota. It has been stained and it is beautiful. Being there, seeing this ship, and learning about its history was very special.

I was thinking, as I walked through the museum and saw all the artifacts, that people are finally learning to save history. Very little remains of the Revolutionary War. We have a lot of artifacts of the Civil War, but nothing compares to all we have from the wars of the 20th Century. In this museum were letters from Commanders to parents of men who were killed, their wallets with their girl's or wife's pictures, clothes, personal items, and many pictures taken of the person. It was that way throughout the ship, whether the person died in battle or survived. The artifacts were very interesting and it was good to have so much history preserved. One of the men who served on the ship left $150,000 in his will for another room to be added in the museum for his artifacts when he died. This room was filled with his history, the history of his mates, and the ship.

We had no idea this Memorial would be so impressive, along with being very interesting. I found myself thinking of our son,

Christopher. After graduating from Villanova University in Philadelphia, he served three years in the United States Navy. He would have thoroughly enjoyed seeing this battleship and learning its history. We are very glad we took the time to visit the U.S. South Dakota Memorial.

The rest of our day was spent driving to the big city! We enjoyed more of the prairie as we drove along. When we got to Minnesota, there were many large farms. They weren't as spread out as they were in South Dakota, Nebraska, and Kansas. They grew corn and many had the equipment on the farms to convert corn to ethanol. There were also many windmills on some of the farms. With the wind in the above states and this part of Minnesota, I would think all of the farms would have these modern windmills. The windmills would certainly create a lot of wind power.

As we got further into Minnesota, we began to see more trees and more small towns. It was nice to see the trees again, until we started hitting a lot of traffic. After that, the road began to look like the Schuylkill Expressway or the Blue Route in Pennsylvania, and I-4 in Florida. We were wishing we were back in the wide-open spaces.

Jim found one more "largest" today – the largest mall. We went to the Mall of America tonight. It is the largest mall in this country. It was four stories tall, filled with one high-end store after another, a food court, and many restaurants. The most unique thing about this mall is that there is an amusement park inside on the first level. The amusement park even has a roller coaster, inside a mall. There were lots of people at the amusement park and lots of people in the mall. We had dinner there and walked around looking at everything. After that, we were content to call it a day and go back to the hotel for a good night's sleep.

Tomorrow we are hoping to see where the movie, "Field of Dreams" was filmed and the Amana colony in Iowa, along with seeing Minneapolis and the Cathedral in that city. I never know, though. Jim is always finding new and different things to do. Me – I am still looking forward to Ashley, Chicago, The Spam Factory (my mom would love it), and The Rock and Roll Hall of Fame.

P.S. Maggie is enjoying this trip as much as us!

Minnesota **The North Star State**
State Motto – The Star of the North
License Plate Saying – 10,000 Lakes

Chapter 15

Yes, there really is a Spam Museum! Come on, you know Spam – the meat in the can from Hormel.

We left Bloomington in a downpour. We wanted to see the City of Minneapolis, but the rain was so bad, we couldn't even see the buildings. That is the way it has been the past three days, rain in the morning, sun in the afternoon, and torrential rains again at night. There has been a lot of flooding.

We decided to ride by the Cathedral Basilica of Saint Mary in Minneapolis. Fortunately, when we got there, the rain stopped and we were able to get out of the car and go inside. We were amazed at how much it looked like our parish church when we were growing up in Philadelphia. We looked at each other and said, "It looks just like Immaculate Conception." The altar was the same, even to the statue of Mary on top of the dome over the altar. It felt like home. The stained-glass windows were the same and in the same places as in Immaculate. The only differences I saw were that there were more altars, more windows, more statues, and the Cathedral was larger. Otherwise, it could have been a carbon copy of our old parish church. Immaculate Conception was built in 1902 and this church was built in 1903. Immaculate was one of the most beautiful churches in Philadelphia. It was second only to the cathedral there. St. Mary's was equally as beautiful, only on a grander scale. We made our three wishes, took pictures, included prayer intentions, and got on our way.

Since it had stopped raining, we went on to St. Paul to see the cathedral there and the capitol building. St. Paul and Minneapolis are called the Twin Cities. They are right next to each other. They are also the only cities that have cathedrals so close to each other. The Bishopric of Minneapolis and St. Paul has two cathedrals, The Cathedral of St. Paul and the Co-Cathedral Basilica of St. Mary in Minneapolis.

The cathedral in St. Paul is called St. Paul's. It began as a log cabin church in 1841. From that it grew into a bigger church, then a bigger church, and it finally became a cathedral as the city grew and the population grew. The cathedral sits high on a hill, which probably makes it look larger. However, it is massive. A pamphlet in the church said that the Statue of Liberty could fit inside it.

The Cathedral was built when the city became a diocese and a bishop was installed. When the cornerstone was laid in 1907, Pope Pius X sent his blessing. He is now a saint and there is a statue of him in the church. There is also an altar of the Pieta and a small chapel surrounding it. Everything in the cathedral was awesome and no expense was spared. It contains 33 different types of marble from 11 countries and four continents. Contained in the main altar are relics of the True Cross, St. Peter, St, Paul, St. Ignatius of Antioch, St. Maria Goretti, and St. Pius X. Again, we made our wishes, prayed for intentions, and took pictures. The Cathedral was wonderful to see. It is difficult to capture its beauty in words. It is a must-see! We are so glad we made the effort to see both of these cathedrals.

We were lucky that the rain stopped; however, when we left the church, the rain started again. It was so heavy, we couldn't get out of the car to see the capitol building. We did drive by, though. The Capitol stood out from all the buildings around it. It was beautiful. Because of the heavy rain, we had to skip the Field of Dreams site. Everything was flooded. We got on our way, hoping to drive out of the rain.

Before leaving, we did drive around the city. There must have been a lot of wealthy people back then. The homes were large and exquisite. They still are today. We saw the home of James J. Hill who expanded the railroad to St. Paul. It was opulent. When he passed away, his fortune was $63 million dollars, and that was back in the 1870's.

Our next stop was the Spam Museum in Austin, Minnesota, the world headquarters of Hormel Foods. The name, "Spam Museum" is on top of a very nice building. We went there on a whim and were greatly surprised. The inside lobby of the museum had ads about Spam over the years. A receptionist greeted us and led us to the theater where we watched a movie about Spam.

Spam came into the market in 1937. It is made of five ingredients: Meat, salt, sugar, water, and a preservative. The meat comes from the shoulder of a pig. It was a staple for the military and Americans during World War II. Since then, Spam has now become a staple for many countries around the world. There are several different varieties of Spam – jalapeno, bacon, cheese, and turkey, to name a few. Mr. Hormel started the company and passed it on to his son who also passed it on to his son. Hormel looked like a good company for employment. We were very impressed with what we learned from the movie.

We moved on to the museum and learned more. The company came up with "Spammy," a sandwich spread. Tons of it were sent to Haiti after the devastation there. It is also being sent to poor and underdeveloped countries around the world to feed the children – FREE. In the museum, we were given samples of the different varieties of Spam. They were good. I also got to try the assembly line. I had to get a can, put the meat in it, put it in the oven, put a label on it, and then put it with the other finished cans. I did it in 33 seconds. Not bad!

Jim and I had a good time at the Spam Museum. We were amazed at all the people who were already there when we arrived. So many visitors come to the Spam Museum that they are now building a bigger museum in the downtown area.

My mom loved Spam. I remember having it often as a child. When I would take her shopping, she always had to get a can of Spam. It didn't matter that she had ten cans already at home. Her philosophy was, "You can never have enough Spam." After she passed, Jim and I were going through the things in her house. We came across this cookie tin high up in the cupboard. Jim got it down and we opened it. The can was filled with the little keys that went around the can of Spam to open it. Jim and I were hysterical laughing when we saw what was in the can. Being of the Depression Era, my mom saved everything. I can just hear her saying, "I need those extra keys in case I lose a key or the one on the can breaks."

Well, Jim found another "largest" today – the spire of St. Paul's Cathedral. Who knows what he will find tomorrow! Me – the Amana Colonies, Ashley, Chicago, and The Rock and Roll Hall of Fame are waiting for me to enjoy. I know I will!

P.S. The baseball field in Austin was completely under water, as were the farmers' fields. They had a bad winter here and it doesn't look like the start of a good summer for the people.

Chapter 16

Today we were treated to sunshine, blue skies, and puffy white clouds. It was a beautiful day to ride and see the Iowa and Illinois countryside.

We began our day at the Brucemore House, one of the outstanding estates in Cedar Rapids, Iowa. It dates back to the 1880's. The house was beautiful and the grounds were even more so. The estate was on a lot of acreage outside the city. The acreage was put to good use for the family. It had a pool, flower garden, book bindery, tennis courts, and an art studio. The house was huge, with porches around the outside of the house. Everything was taken care of so well. Many prominent and important people visited and stayed there as guests of one of the families, including Herbert Hoover, Harry Truman, and Hollywood stars.

Three families lived in the house/estate, the Sinclair's, the Douglas,' and the Hall's, not all at the same time. The first family, the Sinclair's wealth was from meat packing. When the Sinclair's moved out, the Douglas' bought the estate. Their wealth came from Quaker Oats. When the Douglas' moved out, the Hall's bought the estate. Their wealth came from metal products. Mr. Hall invented the rock crusher that gave way to paved roads. He also made metal manhole covers for streets. When Mrs. Hall passed away, she left the estate to the city of Cedar Rapids to preserve for history. The city has done an excellent job in preserving the estate. Mr. Hall's brother was one of the men who perished on the ship Titanic.

From there, we moved on to the Amana Colonies. The colonies were begun by a religious sect from Germany seeking religious

Geneviève Welsh Bottorff

freedom in America. They have been in America since the 1700's. The people first settled in Buffalo, New York, but as the city grew, they wanted more isolation. They bought 26,000 acres outside of Cedar Rapids and began their new colonies there. The people believed in communal living, sharing the profits of their work, living off the land, and trusted that God would bless them for their toils. There are five colonies on the 26,000 acres. Contained in their colonies are their church, school, stores, homes, and farms. They were and still are very successful. Their success also came from Amana refrigeration. They needed something large to store their meat, and they invented the upright food freezer. Amana refrigeration was bought out by Whirlpool, but the colonies still keep the name.

The farms, homes, and land are immaculate and beautiful. We were a little disappointed, though. We thought we were going to see a working colony. Instead there were many shops with their wares and the food they make. The colony reminded me of New Hope, Pennsylvania with all the little shops. We stopped in the bakery and bought some bread and strudel. The strudel was delicious. We bought rhubarb and blackberry strudel. They were so good, we wished we had bought more. Of course, they are all gone. We will have the bread tomorrow. Everything is made from scratch and is made by the people. It was really nice to see, but I would have rather seen a working colony and the food in the making.

We needed to get back on the road and be on our way to Chicago. We drove on back roads all the way. The countryside is beautiful, one farm after another, and corn growing on both sides of the road. There were huge silos on the farms to hold the corn. One farm had so many of the new windmills that we couldn't count all of them. They were blowing rapidly with the wind. The wind is very prevalent in the mid-west.

We passed through Iowa into Illinois and I was surprised to see a very rural Illinois. I didn't expect that. I guess I thought everything was big city. The southern part of Illinois is very rural with beautiful farms and nice little towns. We are spoiled taking the back roads

66

instead of the big highways. We don't like when we have to switch to a major highway. The back roads are so peaceful. The farm settings are pristine. It is refreshing!

As we got closer to Chicago, bigger and very prosperous towns started coming into view. The towns looked like any other modern suburb outside a big city. We didn't get to Chicago today. We are staying outside of Chicago tonight and will get there tomorrow. I have never been to Chicago and I am looking forward to seeing the "Windy City." I can't imagine any place being windier than Kansas and Nebraska. Most of all, we are looking forward to seeing our beautiful granddaughter, Ashley. She is going to be our tour guide.

Jim did it again. He found another largest – "The World's Largest Truck Stop" on Route 80 in Iowa. He even saved his appetite so he could eat there. It is VERY big! For as far as we could see, there were trucks – one truck after another. The truck stop has every restaurant you can imagine inside. There are also gift shops, clothing stores, a children's toy store, general store, and they are all downstairs with the restaurants. Upstairs there is a dentist, a doctor, a chapel, showers, you name it, and it is there. We could have taken a whole day just to look at everything. It was fun to see. I enjoyed looking in all the shops. Jim enjoyed eating and taking pictures of the truck stop.

I know Jim will find more "largest" things to see before this trip is over, but he is also looking forward to seeing Ashley, Notre Dame, and the Ford Museum. Me – I'm going to see Ashley and Chicago tomorrow. That is enough for now!

P.S. Tomorrow we will check into our timeshare for the week – our home away from home. It will be good to settle down in one place for a while.

Iowa   **The Hawkeye State**
         State Motto – "Our Liberties We Prize and Our Rights We Will Maintain"
         License Plate Saying – The Corn State

Chapter 17

We had a great time with our granddaughter, Ashley, and Eric, her fiancé, (now husband). They look wonderful and very happy. Living in Chicago agrees with them, especially in the summer. They live in Edgewater, the northernmost part of Chicago. They live one block from the beach – the beach meaning Lake Michigan. Of course, we immediately went to the beach. Ashley and Eric have paddleboards. They went out on the lake with them and showed us their paddleboard skills. Paddleboards are pretty cool! If it weren't for alligators in the lakes in Florida, Jim and I would get them, too.

Lake Michigan is very, very large. If I didn't know it was a lake, I would have thought I was at the ocean. I have never seen a lake that big. It completely surrounds the downtown area of Chicago. There were even little waves rippling on the shore. A beach surrounds the lake. Growing up at the Jersey shore, Ashley loves being so close to the beach. There were a lot of people on the beach, paddleboarders in the water and many boats. We walked around the lake and stopped for lunch at a restaurant on the beach. Fun!

Eric had to leave us at 2:00 pm to go to work. We missed having him with us. Ashley took us to several towns; Lincoln Park, Evanston, and Edgewater. They are very nice towns. We saw Loyola University and Northwestern University in Evanston.

Evanston is a beautiful town. We saw many large and gorgeous homes in the town. There is also a main street with a lot of shops and restaurants. Northwestern University is very big. It was graduation day and we got to see the graduates and their families going to graduation. That was very nice to see the students in their caps and gowns. They looked so nice.

We drove through Chicago and from what I saw riding in the car, it looks like a nice city. The buildings were surrounded in fog. I am hoping the weather will be clear tomorrow. We will get to see more of the city tomorrow.

We are now settled into our timeshare for the night. The condo is very nice and very spacious. It overlooks a river and the view is beautiful. We have a two-bedroom unit. The other bedroom turned out to be a complete unit in itself with a kitchen, bathroom, bedroom, and living room. Yeah, we can really spread out for a few days.

Jim did get to see another "largest" today – my lip. Ashley was taking me to see the B'hai Temple. I tripped going up the many steps and went flying. I hit my head, nose, and the side of my face on the steps. I also cut my knees, hands, fingers, and legs. My tooth went through my lip and my lip is very LARGE. For just tripping, I did a great job with cuts and bruises. Thank God for all those prayers for our safety in the various churches because I really am fine. Amen for prayers. I didn't break my nose. My face didn't swell. I don't have a black eye. My tooth didn't break. I didn't have to go to the hospital. My cuts and bruises will heal and I will be fine. It that's the worst that happens on this trip, it's okay. Besides, I'm so glad that I could provide Jim with a "largest" for the day!!!

Tomorrow, we will explore more of Chicago. I am looking forward to that. Jim is still waiting for Notre Dame and the Ford Museum. Me – The Rock and Roll Hall of Fame and whatever else we can see between here and Ohio. Jim mentioned going to Mackinac Island in Michigan. That would be wonderful!

Illinois   The Prairie State
       State Motto – "State Sovereignty, National Union"
       License Plate Saying – Land of Lincoln

Chapter 18

Jim and I had a wonderful day touring the "Windy City." Chicago is a beautiful city. Contrary to popular belief, it is not windy. We learned that Chicago is called the "Windy City" because of the politicians – they are windy. They talk too much. I never knew that.

We met Ashley at Navy Pier and began our day. Navy Pier is sort of like Fisherman's Wharf in San Francisco. It is on Lake Michigan and goes out into the lake. On the pier there are shops, museums, restaurants, art galleries, and boats to rent to go sightseeing. It was great walking on the pier and looking at everything.

On the Pier, we visited a museum of stained glass windows that came from churches that have been closed and houses that have been destroyed. A lot of them were Tiffany stained glass. The scenes on the windows were outstanding. One window has a scene of the Annunciation. It depicted Mary, the Blessed Mother, and the Angel Gabriel when the angel appeared to her. If I stood close to the window, I could clearly see the angel. When I stood back from the window, the angel was white and filmy in sort of a heavenly haze. That was amazing. I have never seen anything like that – a stained glass window that changed color and showed another dimension. Incredible!

From the Pier, we went to Grant Park, where there was an art festival. It was interesting walking around and looking at the art. Of course, there was lots of food. You can't have a festival without food. In the park, there was a beautiful fountain. I commented on how nice it was. Ashley told me it was very much like a fountain in Paris. Jim sat and looked at the boats in Lake Michigan while Ashley and I walked all over the area. We went to Millennium Park and I saw The Bean sculpture. The Bean sculpture is like a big shiny ball. We could see ourselves in it and I took a picture of us standing in front of the Bean with our reflection in the background. We kept walking and saw other sculptures. One sculpture we approached from the back and I thought it was an ear of corn. When we walked around to the front, I saw that it was the face of a woman. Her features couldn't be seen from the back of the sculpture. It was very different, but intriguing

When we were on Navy Pier, it was so foggy we could hardly see the water, let alone the city. When we got to the parks, the sun was shining beautifully. The large buildings were clearly visible then. They were a beautiful sight to see. Many apartment buildings and condos are across the street from Lake Michigan. The people living in them have an outstanding view.

What impressed me the most about Chicago was how the people make such great use of their resources. Wherever we went, wherever I looked, I saw Chicagoans enjoying this beautiful day. People were on the beach and in their boats on Lake Michigan. They were bike riding, walking, jogging, skating, walking babies, at Navy Pier, in the city parks, or swimming in Lake Michigan. That's not a scene I see occurring in other big cities. I thought it was wonderful. I liked Chicago. I thought it was a very cool city.

Eric had to work, so Ashley was our tour guide again today. She should get a job as a tour guide. She was really good. We ended the day with a wonderful dinner together in one of her favorite restaurants. I hated to leave my beautiful, grown-up granddaughter. It was hard to say goodbye. I hope she and Eric plan a trip to Florida soon!

On our way out of the city, we drove by McCormick Place. It is the largest convention center in the United States with 2,600,000 square feet of space. The Convention Center in Orlando, FL is the second largest convention center with 2,100,000 square feet. I'm glad that Jim got his "largest" for the day.

We had a wonderful day in Chicago. I'd like to go back another time and see more of the city. I am sure we will. Right now, it is time to move on. Jim can't wait to see the Ford Museum. Me – Mackinac Island and the Rock and Roll Hall of Fame are still calling my name!

P.S. I am healing nicely. My lip isn't nearly as big as it was yesterday.

Chapter 19

What a lovely day Jim and I had today. We spent the afternoon in Naperville, Illinois visiting my neighbor from Stafford Street in Philadelphia, Jerry, and his wife, Jane. It was great seeing Jerry again and meeting Jane. We had a good time talking about our childhood on the streets of Philadelphia, catching up on each other's news and travels, and filling each other in on old neighbors and what is happening with them. Jerry and I have known each other since I was five and he was seven. We had a lot of stories to share with Jim and Jane.

Jerry and Jane showed us around Naperville. It is a great town. We had a delicious lunch and then walked around the downtown area. They have a lot of sculptures around the town. We saw a sculpture of The Cat in The Hat, Dick Tracy, and a fountain that looked just like a dandelion, among others. I commented on what the fountain looked like and was told that the name of it is The Dandelion. There is a river that runs through the downtown with a covered walking bridge to the other side. It was so picturesque.

They took us for a ride around the town. The homes are beautiful – a lot of big old houses, which I loved, and new construction homes that blend right in with old. Their home is new and it is gorgeous, as well as being as warm and gracious as Jerry and Jane.

Jane told me that the population of the town has doubled since they moved there 27 years ago. I can see why. If you are looking for the perfect little town to settle in, Naperville is definitely a town to check out. Thank you, Jerry and Jane, for a wonderful afternoon.

After we left Jerry and Jane, we did something rare, we went back to the timeshare and just relaxed. That was a nice change. It felt good! We haven't had too many nights like that. The condo is very nice. I hate to leave it tomorrow, but there are "... places to see and miles to go before I sleep."

You know, this isn't such a bad life. We stay at hotels. The beds are ready and comfortable. We sleep and wake up refreshed. The hotels have free breakfast that is ready for us in the morning. We use the hotel's laundry room to do our wash. Our day consists of driving, doing something fun or seeing something interesting, enjoying a good dinner, and going to a hotel with beds ready for us, and the same scenario plays out the next day. Pretty good life! I think we both could get used to this.

Tomorrow we are off to Dearborn, MI. I've heard so much about Michigan. I am anxious to see it. Jim is eagerly looking forward to the Ford Museum and Greenfield Village. Me – I'm still waiting for The Grand Hotel and The Rock and Roll Hall of Fame!

P.S. Hmm, I think I'll go fall into that comfy bed! It's looking very inviting.

Chapter 20

Michigan is beautiful. I know, I know, I always say I think the state or town is beautiful. I am repetitive, but they really are beautiful. I would compare driving in Michigan to driving on the Northeast Extension of the turnpike in Pennsylvania – lots of trees and rolling hills. We saw many farms and as we got closer to a city, many more brick houses. Brick seems to be prevalent in the mid-west.

As I said before, we are not traveling on major highways. We are mostly going on back roads enabling us to see the countryside. I'm glad we are seeing the little towns and byways across the country. It's refreshing to know that small town America still exists.

The Henry Ford Museum is in Dearborn, MI. We are staying outside of Dearborn in Canton. I am sure that there are many interesting things to see in Detroit, but we are not planning to go there. We got lost because of a road closure and ended up outside of Detroit. The section we were in was like a war zone. I know there are sections like that in every city. However, 90% of the homes we saw were made of brick, needing very little maintenance. Most of the homes we saw were boarded up, windows smashed, doors falling off, debris everywhere, and roofs caving in. I'm sure they could be fixed and with a little bit of care, they would last a long time. That is all that is needed. With the influx of foreign cars, Detroit lost a lot of business and jobs. The jobs haven't come back. I am sure that the poverty level has a lot to do with the neglect of homes and neighborhoods. It is very sad to see once great cities in such condition.

The homes here are different from the homes in the East. In Philadelphia where we grew up, there is street after street and row after row of homes that are connected to each other. In all the big cities we have been in, I have yet to see row houses like there are in Philadelphia. Here there are rows of houses, but the houses are not connected. They are single family homes and looked like they were once very nice homes. I saw very few connected row homes, even in the section I described above. Most were single family homes on tree-lined streets, with a little ground around them. That is really nice. People in the East would love to have homes like that. I guess because land is so plentiful here, people could afford to build cities like that. However, I just don't understand the concept of neglect. If you are lucky enough to have a nice home, you take care of it. I was shocked by what I saw. It is the Irish in me, the love of home and land.

On the bright side, I have liked what I have seen of Michigan. Canton, Dearborn, Ann Arbor, all are very nice cities. There is also so much to do and see here. I wish we had more time. Flowers were plentiful and visible everywhere. There were beautiful hanging baskets on every lamppost. For a state that sees six months of bad winters, it really comes alive with color in the summer. I could smell the flowers and sweet clover wherever we went.

Jim's day is coming tomorrow, the Henry Ford Museum awaits. Jim has been waiting for this since the beginning of the trip. Everything we have heard and read about it says it is amazing. I'm sure Jim will find another "largest" there. Me – I am looking forward to seeing the museum, too, but The Grand Hotel and The Rock and Roll Hall of Fame are still calling my name.

P.S. Maggie wants you to know that she hasn't roared once in 20 days. She is very proud of us!

Chapter 21

The Henry Ford Museum is everything we have heard about and more. It is AMAZING! We loved every minute of being there. We were there the whole day and still didn't see all of it. We are going back tomorrow.

You would not believe all there is in this museum. To name a few – the limo President Kennedy was riding in when he was shot; the chair President Lincoln was sitting in at Ford's Theater when he was assassinated; Teddy Roosevelt's brougham; the bus Rosa Parks sat in during the Civil Rights Movement; the original Oscar Meyer Weiner mobile; an original diner; an original steam train; race cars, old cars, more cars, including the Model T; planes; old and valuable furniture; farm equipment; musical instruments; doll houses; clocks – and they are all original. Henry Ford collected things from all over and the Ford Foundation has carried on this tradition.

It was unbelievable to see President Lincoln's chair, with the blood stains still visible. I just stood there looking at it, in awe that it still existed. The limo that carried President Kennedy has been completely redone since that time and was used by Presidents, Johnson, Nixon, Ford, and Clinton. Still, having lived through President Kennedy's assassination it was an incredible feeling to actually see that limo up close and personal. I never dreamed the exact bus that Rosa Parks sat in would be in a museum. I was able to go on the bus and sit exactly where she sat when she refused to give up her seat to a white man. I could feel her brave spirit and her tiredness that day. History came alive!

There are also areas within the museum on the Revolutionary War, the Civil War, the Women's Suffragist Movement, and the Civil Rights Movement. They were incredible! Each museum told the history of these events. There were pictures, videos, artifacts, and original footage where possible. I learned a lot. I thought I knew a lot about our history, but there was so much more to learn. I really did not know much about the Women's Suffragist Movement. I found it shocking what was done to women at that time. What they went through and suffered to gain the right to vote was terrible. They were heroic women!

The museum is huge. It must take up several city blocks. The whole building is made of brick. The front of the museum is a replica of Independence Hall in Philadelphia. There is an IMAX theater inside the museum. The museum hallways are outstanding, with crystal chandeliers hanging from the ceilings. There are three restaurants inside the museum, one of them being the diner. I have never seen such a spectacular museum. I am sure that there is nothing else like this in the world.

The fact that almost all of the contents in the museum are original, makes the Henry Ford Museum truly unique. There were actual cars from the time Ford first started making them. Cars from then until present day are all on display. We had a Studebaker back in the 50's, and sure enough, there was a Studebaker just like my dad's. My boyfriend back then picked me up from high school in his family's '59 Plymouth. I saw one just like it in the museum. That brought back fun memories. There are race cars throughout the years, horse-drawn trolleys, the first truck, the first school bus, stagecoaches, and wagons. There was even an 18-wheeler in the building.

There are many different sections in the museum. I went into the one on furniture. The furniture I saw was beautiful. There was living room furniture, bedroom furniture, kitchen furniture, and dining room furniture – all original. The furniture was either donated to the museum or purchased by Henry Ford. The tables, chairs, dressers, china closets, and dollhouses were incredible in detail. Most were hand made by very skilled craftsmen. The dollhouses belonged to little girls of long ago. They were very elaborate, with many rooms and handmade furniture for each room. I loved my dollhouse when I was a child and thought it was beautiful. My dollhouse was no comparison to these wonderful dollhouses.

One section of the museum held farm equipment. The equipment, including a tractor, was inside the building. There were plows from very early in our country and a history plaque that covered how each generation improved on farm machinery. It was very interesting. Henry Ford was an admirer of George Washington Carver and a whole part of this section was devoted to him and his contribution to farming and working the land.

Another section of the museum traced telling time from the sun dial to modern day electricity. I learned more about clocks and their beginnings than I ever knew. Clocks in the 1700's and 1800's were mostly made in New England. They were beautiful and usually only owned by the wealthy of that time. The clocks were in a very nice, ornately decorated wood cabinet. Under the clock on the cabinet door would be a beautiful scene of winter or summer or nature. I was very impressed with them because they were so pretty.

I went into the television (TV) section. It traced the beginning of televisions to what they are today. There were TV's on and they were showing different TV shows of that time: Howdy Doody, Ed Sullivan, The Big Circus, and many more. Each decade from the 50's on had its own TV and the shows of that decade were playing on the TV. I thought back to when we got our first TV. It was in 1950. It had a very small screen in a very large cabinet. It didn't matter how small the screen was, we didn't care. We were watching TV and it was thrilling. Howdy Doody was my favorite show when I was a child. It was wonderful to sit there, watch, and remember. Great memories!

The museum closed at 5:00 o'clock and I hadn't yet gotten to the section on planes and music. We are going back tomorrow to see Greenfield Village, the outdoor part of the museum. That is supposed to take all day, too. The Henry Ford Museum is a MUST-SEE. Treat yourself to a very special day and go visit!

Jim was a happy man today. He loved the museum. He got to see the "most powerful steam railroad engine," the Allegheny Locomotive. It, too, is inside the building. It is huge. Jim went on the engine, checked it out, blew the train whistle, and came out smiling. You gotta' love this man!

Jim is now ready for Part 2 of the museum, Greenfield Village. Me – I want to see it, too, and then on to the Grand Hotel and The Rock and Roll Hall of Fame. I'm ready!

Chapter 22

Greenfield Village was wonderful. We went there for the whole day and, again, did not see all of it. Back in the 1930's, Henry Ford created this village. He wanted it to be an original working American village. It is unique in that it contains as many of the original things as he could get. For instance, his boyhood home is here. He moved his house to the village and proceeded to furnish it as it was when he was a boy.

The village is huge. It covers 240 acres. It is also a true working village, as it was at the turn of the century. There are two farms, one for animals and one for agriculture. When I walked into the village, I came upon the blacksmith, millinery, glass blower, tinsmith, general store, dressmaker and carpenter, newspaper, grain mill, and pottery shops. As I went into each one, the person was working at his/her trade and ready to share what he/she was doing and also demonstrate how it is done. All the shops are the original shops that once lined the streets of America in different cities. They were bought by Henry Ford and transported to this village.

The dressmaker had a huge loom and was weaving. She told us that she wasn't making dresses at this time of year. She was making her woolens for the coming winter. She also told us that it takes three days to thread the spindles on the loom with the different woolen threads. If you want a color woven in, that has to be done with a hand threaded shuttle that you weave through the cloth. If the loom isn't threaded right, everything has to be taken down and you have to start all over. She works the loom with her feet. It was fascinating to watch how weaving is done. Hanging all over the shop were blankets, towels, and other items that she made. The wool is obtained from the sheep they raise at the farm.

In the glass blower's shop, he showed us how he made glass Christmas ornaments. There were several hot kilns along the walls and the shop was very warm. Imagine that job on a hot summer day! He had a long poker that he dipped in liquid then held in the kiln for a few minutes. After taking it out of the kiln, he used several tools to shape the ornament, putting it back in the kiln after each adjustment. When the ornament was shaped the way he wanted it, he put it inside a warming block while he made the top of the ornament. The warming block kept the ornament from getting cold and losing its shape. The glass blower then got more liquid on the poker, put it in the kiln for a few seconds, then brought it to the warming block. I watched as hot liquid was poured over the top of the ornament. From this hot liquid, he shaped the top of the ornament so it could hang on a Christmas tree. The ornament then had to be baked, cooled, and decorated. The finished ornament was very nice.

At the print shop, the printer picked some of the children out of the group of visitors and showed them how to set the type to print something. The type was so small and it had to be set backwards so it would be readable when printed. That is very tedious work. He showed the children how to fix the type on the printer and what had to be done in order to print something. The printer was very large and everything had to be done by hand. The children were fascinated, as were we, and they got to keep what they printed. The man then rolled up their paper, put a ribbon around it, and the children happily walked out of the print show with something they printed themselves.

It was that way with every shop we went in; they were working and teaching shops. We learned so much. The Village reminded me of Williamsburg and Jamestown in Virginia, only 100% better and larger. I have seen demonstrations at both of these places and they were good, but nothing was on such a grand scale as it is here. The interaction between the people and the workers here was in much greater depth. It was fascinating and interesting at the same time.

There are different sections of the Village. When we finished seeing the working town, we went on to the countryside and the homes. The homes were beautiful and, unbelievably, they were the original homes of the people. Some of the homes belonged to Noah Webster, Stephen Foster, Thomas Edison, George Washington Carver, William Holmes McGuffey who created easy-to-read school books ("Dick saw Jane," etc.), the Wright Brothers, and many more homes. Each home was furnished as it would have been in that day.

Among the other buildings in the Village were a church, school, Meeting Hall, Town Hall, restaurant and inn, slave quarters, and log cabins. All of these buildings, along with the houses, were transported from their original sites to Greenfield Village by Henry Ford. Ford was such an admirer of Thomas Edison, he not only had his house in the Village, he also had his laboratory. Along with Ford's house, there was his workshop and a building showing how his assembly line worked. The Wright Brothers shop was right in back of their bicycle shop. The whole Village was incredible – totally incredible!

The church in the Village was transported from a little town in Connecticut. It looked just like the church where my daughter, Genny, was married in Vermont. It was just a small white church with wooden pews inside, but it was beautiful in its simplicity. The church was so similar, in my mind's eye, I could see Genny and Eric on that altar, just like on the day they were married. A beautiful memory!

The Village closed at 5:00 o'clock. Of course, we hadn't seen everything. We didn't even get to the farms. We really needed three days to see everything; one for the museum, one for the Village, and one to go back to both to see what we missed. It was another wonderful day. I could go on and on, writing volumes about the

Village and the museum. However, this really is a MUST-SEE! Mere words don't do it justice.

This day was not without its "largest." The Henry Ford Museum and Greenfield Village is the largest indoor/outdoor museum complex in the United States. Jim loved the whole experience. His dream of seeing them came true. Me – I loved them, too, but now I'm ready for The Grand and The Rock and Roll Hall of Fame. Tomorrow!

P.S. I don't know, Jim said something about going to see the largest hamburger tomorrow. Do you really think there could be such a thing?!

Michigan – **The Great Lake State**
State Motto – "If you seek a pleasant peninsula, look about you"
License Plate Saying – Great Lake State

Chapter 23

No, we didn't find the world's largest hamburger today. Instead, we found the world's largest hot dog. Can you believe that?!

We left Dearborn, Michigan, and headed north to The Grand Hotel in Mackinac Island. It was an eight-hour drive – a very long drive, but The Grand Hotel is something I want to see very much.

On the way, we stopped in Holland, Michigan. Holland is known for its Dutch heritage. Every year in May, just like its namesake, tulips abound here. This year was their 88th Tulip Festival. We missed seeing the Festival, but I was told the tulips are beautiful. I know we would have enjoyed that. However, we did go to the DeKlomp Wooden Shoe and Delft Factory, where we watched wooden shoes being made. That was interesting. There were samples of wooden shoes in every size, color, and decoration we could want in the Gallery. We did try shoes on. Jim thought they were comfortable. I couldn't imagine wearing them all day, but they were fun to try on and walk around. They weren't as heavy as I thought they would be.

We also saw Delftware being made. Delftware is so pretty. I have always admired it, but didn't know that is what it is called. Delftware is pottery that is white with blue designs on it. Liquid clay is poured into molds, fired in kilns, and when cool, hand-painted by artists in signature-blue Dutch designs. It is so beautiful. There were many offerings including dishes, bowls, vases, pitchers, candlesticks, one more beautiful than the other. I am very sorry that I didn't buy anything. I would have loved to have had one of the pieces. Opportunity lost!

After leaving Holland, we continued on our way. We were driving to Mackinaw City where we were staying for the night. Mackinaw City is across from Mackinac Island. The only way to get to Mackinac Island is by ferry from Mackinaw City. We walked around the city, looked in the shops, and had dinner in a large log cabin restaurant on the banks of Lake Michigan. Dinner was delicious; just what we needed after a long day in the car.

Having never seen one of the great lakes, I am in awe at the size of Lake Michigan. I saw it in Chicago and it was with us all the way to the top of the state of Michigan. It is a lake and it is immense. From the ferry dock in Mackinaw City, we saw Mackinac Island. We were told that there are huge barge/ships on Lake Michigan that chop through the ice on the lake so it can still be traversed in winter. Amazing!

When we were walking back from the restaurant to our hotel, we passed by a diner. In front of the diner was a sign saying, "World's Largest Hot Dog," with an arrow pointing up. We both looked up and there on the roof of the diner was the world's largest hot dog, complete with hot dog roll and all the condiments. Who knew?! Jim didn't. We looked at each other and started laughing at the irony of this finding. All the other "largest," Jim planned our trip around seeing them. We drove through little towns on back roads to get there. Here, without even looking our path crosses with another largest. And, Jim loves hot dogs. He was a happy man tonight!

We are now settled down for the night. It was a good day and I know tomorrow is going to be even better. Jim is content. Me – I can't wait to see the Grand Hotel.

P.S. Finding the World's Largest Hot Dog today was quite a fun surprise!

Chapter 24

Ever since I read the book and saw the movie, "Somewhere in Time," I have wanted to see the Grand Hotel. I loved the movie and the book. The setting of the book and the movie is the Grand Hotel in Mackinac Island.

"Somewhere in Time" is the story of a young playwriter, Richard Collier (played by Christopher Reeves) and an actress, Elise McKenna (played by Jane Seymour). Richard lives in the 1970's and Elise lived in the late 18th century and the 19th century. Burned out in his writing, Richard goes to The Grand Hotel seeking rest and perspective. A room in the hotel contains pictures, books, and artifacts of earlier days. There is a picture of Elise in that room. Richard is exploring the room and his eyes are drawn to the picture of Elise. He is captivated by the woman in the picture. Richard can't take his eyes off her and, through the picture, he falls in love with Elise. Richard is in present day 1971 for him and the picture of Elise was taken in 1896. He wants to go back in time to meet her. What happens when he does is a captivating story that can only be appreciated by reading the book or seeing the movie. It is a beautiful story.

We booked our ferry passage and set out across Lake Michigan for Mackinac Island. The ferry was full. There is seating inside the ferry and outside on the top deck. We chose the top deck. It was a beautiful ride. It was sunny but windy. I found the wind refreshing.

The town of Mackinac Island is beautiful and quaint. It looks like an old seashore resort town. There are no cars permitted on the island. Everything is brought there by ferry. Only horse and buggies are allowed on the roads. There were fancy horse and buggies, trolleys pulled by horses, touring buses pulled by horses, trucks pulled by horses, even the Federal Express truck was pulled by a horse. There were also bicycles so tourists and locals could bike around the town. The town included several hotels, many eateries, fudge shops, ice cream parlors, stores, and souvenir shops. Before we went to The Grand Hotel, we had lunch, walked around the town, and enjoyed everything we saw.

We could have gone to the Grand by horse and buggy, but chose to walk. It was quite a sight walking up the hill and catching my first glimpse of the hotel. The Grand sits high on a hill, overlooking Lake Michigan. It is everything I thought it would be and more. It is exquisite, elegant, and commanding. It is huge, with a porch that wraps around the exterior. The porch is covered with yellow and white awnings. On the porch are white rocking chairs, wicker furniture and tables. Waiters were bringing drinks and food out on the porch for the patrons. American flags hung at two-foot intervals across the porch. It was quite an impressive sight.

The outside steps of the Grand are covered in red carpeting, so beautiful against the white of the Hotel. There was a doorman/greeter on duty to open the door for visitors and patrons. Since Jim is the doorman/greeter at the Boardwalk Resort in Disney World, we had to get his picture with the doorman. We also had to get our picture taken in the rocking chairs, sitting on the porch. The doorman took our picture and we had a grand time talking to him about what it was like to work there. He told us that he loved what he was doing.

For a $20 fee, we could go into the hotel. Of course, we paid the fee and eagerly went to see the inside of the hotel. The inside was immaculate and very luxurious. There were plush sofas, chairs, and tables set up all around the parlor level. There was a bustle of activity inside the hotel. People were having "high tea," which was offered to all for $45. There are several restaurants and bars in the hotel besides the main dining room. The hotel is also home to a theater, art gallery, business center, Gerald R. Ford Conference Room, and many shops. The main dining room is very elegant. It is decorated in green and white; green plush chairs, white woodwork and tablecloths, and window treatments with various colors and trimmed in green. The windows were floor to ceiling, with views of the grounds and Lake Michigan. It looked just like it did in the movie. Quite a spectacle! I can only imagine how good the food must be.

We walked around the inside of the hotel and saw everything there was so see, including the theater which was beautiful. We then went outside and walked around the grounds. The grounds were magnificent with many gardens – Margaret's Garden, Front Street Gardens, Pool Gardens, Wedding Garden, Tea Garden, Triangle Garden, Horseshoe Garden, Tennis Gardens, along with Wildflower Hill. All were taken care of very well. I saw many different varieties of flowers, all flourishing grandly, everywhere I looked. It was a spectacular sight. Also on the grounds were a labyrinth, walking trail, golf course, tennis courts, and a swimming complex.

We were told that "back in the day," there were four grand hotels, and that the Grand was one of them. The other three are The Greenbrier in West Virginia, The Breakers in Florida, and The Broadmore in Colorado. We also learned that several U. S. Presidents and many noted dignitaries stayed at The Grand Hotel over the years. There were pictures of them in the hotel.

The history of the hotel was very interesting. In 1886 The Michigan Central Railroad, the Grand Rapids and Indiana Railroad, and the Detroit and Cleveland Steamship Navigation Company joined together and formed the Mackinac Island Hotel Group. They wanted to bring tourism to the Island and commissioned the building of the Grand Hotel for that purpose. They wanted the hotel built in 90 days. Laborers worked round the clock to accomplish this. The Hotel was completed in 93 days and opened on July 10, 1887.

The Grand Hotel lived up to my every expectation. It was quite a sight to see. I am so glad we included this in our journey. We learned that the Grand is the World's Largest Summer Hotel and that it has the World's Longest Front Porch. Jim enjoyed seeing the hotel and learning these facts. The day was not without a "largest." However, I am the happy person today! One of my dreams came to fruition. I saw The Grand Hotel; sat on those wonderful rocking chairs on the porch enjoying the view; relived the movie in the sights I saw; and walked in the footsteps of many prominent people who graced this hotel with their presence. Wonderful!

Tomorrow we start on the last round of our trip across America. We head to Ohio and The Rock and Roll Hall of Fame. YEAH!

Chapter 25

On our way to The Rock and Roll Hall of Fame, we drove through Indiana. When we first talked about taking this trip, we planned to spend some time at Notre Dame. Because of time constraints and including other places along the way, that didn't happen. Since we were going through Indiana on our way to Ohio, we decided to at least do a drive-by of Notre Dame. It wasn't what we wanted, but it was better than not seeing it at all.

The University of Notre Dame is located in South Bend, Indiana. Their nickname is the "Fighting Irish." Being of Irish descent, we were raised loving Notre Dame. Jim followed their football games religiously, as did our fathers, so it was important to us to see it.

The campus is huge and beautiful with large trees, very large grassy areas, and prolific with many varieties of flowers. Some students were playing soccer on one of the grassy areas, others were playing rugby in another area, and still others were playing football. Many students were laying out in the grassy areas studying or just hanging out. There were students everywhere I looked, and still plenty of room for more activities.

On the campus, there are also beautiful old stone buildings, statues, altars, dorms and a large chapel. Walking from one to the other was a trek, and there was still room for more growth. The campus is that big. I didn't get to see everything, but what I did see was wonderful.

I went into the chapel. It was magnificent. There were white marble columns with gold at the top. Ribbons of white marble carried on to the large domed ceiling. The ceiling was blue with cherubs/angels painted on the blue ceiling with shining stars coming from each angel's hands. The altar was beautiful. There was an arch over it that reached up to the ceiling. There were more paintings above the altar, stained glass windows, lights hanging down from the ceiling, and touches of gold everywhere. I was in awe of the beauty my eyes beheld.

Many people were in the chapel praying. I knelt to pray, also. I made my three wishes and included others' intentions. It was such a special moment to actually be in the chapel at Notre Dame. It is a moment I will never forget.

Jim and I did make it to Notre Dame, after all. A dream we have had for a long time to see it came true. It was too short, but maybe we will get back again when we have more time. Nothing "biggest" today, just total awe at what we saw and gratitude that we were given this opportunity. God is so good!

Onward to The Rock and Roll Hall of Fame! Jim and I can't wait!

Indiana – **The Hoosier State**
State Motto – "The Crossroads of America"
License Plate Saying – Crossroads of America

Chapter 26

WOW!!! The Rock and Roll Hall of Fame was WONDERFUL! It exceeded both our expectations. I was wishing our son, Mark, were with us. He would have been out of his mind with joy at all they have here.

The Rock and Roll Hall of Fame is in Cleveland, Ohio. It sits on the banks of Lake Erie, along with a science center and other museums. It is a big triangular shaped building made of glass. It is beautiful and the backdrop of Lake Erie enhances its beauty.

There are seven floors to the museum. Each floor contains different memorabilia related to Rock and Roll. The first floor was about the beginning of Rock and Roll. I can still remember being on the Wilson Line (a boat in Philadelphia) with a friend and her mother. We were going across the Delaware River to New Jersey. I was about 12 at the time. A jukebox was playing the song, "Rock Around the Clock" by Bill Haley and the Comets. My friend and I started to jitterbug and it was so much fun. That song was part of the beginning of Rock and Roll. This was my time, my generation, and we ushered in Rock and Roll, the jitterbug, and the twist.

Over the years, I completely forgot about this, but I was reminded today. Adults were very much against Rock and Roll. The first floor of the museum touched on this and I remembered. Parents, ministers, priests, rabbis,' teachers, etc., condemned it as "Music of Satan," "Evil, coming right from the devil." I am sitting here smiling as I write this because it is now coming back to me so clearly. I have to admit that I have said the same thing about the music of today and heavy metal. I'm glad I had this reminder today. However, our lyrics were clean, understandable, spoke of nice things, and we LOVED to dance. That was one of the first things that attracted me to Jim, he was/is a great dancer. I don't think this generation or future generations will ever know how special it is to dance a slow dance to beautiful lyrics with someone you love.

On the first floor, there was also a whole exhibit and film on Elvis. They even had Elvis' motorcycle. There were exhibits of others who also contributed and influenced Rock and Roll. I'm talking about Buddy Holly, Chuck Berry, Fats Domino, Little Richard, The Everly Brothers, Chubby Checker, Jerry Lee Lewis, and so many, many more. There were artifacts from all of them – guitars, costumes, rings, suits, letters, and songs they wrote. I had to read everything and check everything out.

The second floor was about The Beatles, the British Invasion, the Jackson Five, the Supremes, women who contributed to the music – it covered everyone, including instruments, clothing, and memorabilia. There was a film about the Beatles and that was great. In one theater, there was special tribute to Dick Clark and American Bandstand. I think Dick Clark did more and gave more to the growth of Rock and Roll than even the performers. Growing up in Philadelphia, I went to American Bandstand. It was fun. Dick Clark had the performers live on his show, exposing them to the public, and giving them the boost they needed to promote their songs and music. I watched Bandstand every afternoon on TV and I remember so many of the performers on the show. Neil Diamond got his start on Bandstand, along with Paul Anka, Frankie Avalon, Fabian, Bobby Rydell, Chubby Checker, Brenda Lee, Connie Francis and many others. Frankie, Fabian, and Bobby were local boys so of course they were bound to be a success. The movie/tribute was great. I could have watched that all day.

A tribute to Motown was on the third floor. That was great. I loved seeing the Supremes' costumes, all the pictures, and memorabilia.

The music was dancing music and Jim and I danced through that floor and on to the next. I read about the history of Motown and the different performers. That was very interesting, how one man, Barry Gordy, began a new wave of music and put Motown on the map.

As we moved up the floors, each one contained something special about Rock and Roll. We were captivated with each display, each movie, and all there was to see. The fourth floor held a theater that showed a movie about all the inductees of the past 25 years and when each one was honored. That film was wonderful. We could have stayed there all day watching it, we enjoyed it so much. Each time a song or a person come on that we liked and enjoyed back in our younger years, we just smiled at each other and held hands. Some of the songs had so much meaning for us. As we came out of the theater, the walls were covered with the signatures of all the honorees since 1986 when the museum opened. It was just SO cool!

The next floor had an exhibition of what it would have been like to go to one of the music festivals, like Woodstock. We would have loved to have been there, so that was interesting and fun to see. I don't think I would have lasted through rain, mud, no food, etc., but who knows. Things like that don't matter when you are young and having fun.

One floor was about heavy metal and the music that came after the hippies of the 70's. Groups that my children listened to that I didn't like at that time, I have a greater appreciation of now. I can't believe I'm saying that, let alone putting it in writing, but it is true. My son, Mark, took me to see Steely Dan one night when the band was in Philadelphia. That is a whole other story ("A Date with My Son and Steely Dan"), but Mark, I now understand why you liked them so much. When Steely Dan came on, I cheered for you and me.

Each floor had something special to see, things you would not ordinarily see. For instance: Van Halen's drums; film footage that had never been seen before of the groups; why the Beatles picked the names they did for their albums; how Elvis put his heart and soul into his work and his performances; and so much more. We learned personal things about the performers that we would never have known. I appreciate these performers and their music more than I did before. I feel like I have gotten to know them on a personal level since being to this museum. It was very special.

This was such a FUN day! Jim and I are so glad we went. We sang, we danced, we smiled from the time we went in the building until long after we left. It was a wonderful feeling, kind of reliving our youth. Being there with Jim and being able to share this together made it even more spectacular. Even now as I am writing this, I am smiling remembering how much fun it was. The Rock and Roll Hall of Fame is great. It's another must-see!

Tomorrow, we head home. I'm sure Jim will find a "largest" along the way. Me – I can't imagine anything better than what I experienced today. I am a happy woman!

P.S. I haven't heard any more about the largest hamburger.

Ohio   **– The Buckeye State**
State Motto – "With God, All Things Are Possible"
License Plate Saying – Birthplace of Aviation

Chapter 27

WOW, did Maggie growl when we got in the car today and she looked so sad. She was not a happy lion. Then, I looked at Jim and he looked so sad. He was not a happy man. I asked him what was wrong. He said, "I can't believe our vacation is over." With that Maggie growled more. I looked at them both and said, "This isn't the end. We will go on more vacations and we'll see a lot more things." Maggie stopped growling. Jim's smile came back on his face. He was a happy man again. Jeez, what you have to do to keep a lion and a man happy!

On that note, we left beautiful Ohio and headed to Pennsylvania. I had never been in Ohio and I thought it was a great state. I liked everything I saw. I didn't see mountains like there are in Pennsylvania, probably because we didn't go that way. The land was pretty flat the way we went. Seeing Lake Erie was great. It is another one of the Great Lakes that goes on and on. Cleveland made great use of Lake Erie's beauty in building several museums on its banks. The view from the museums was spectacular.

When we crossed the line from Ohio, the mountains of Pennsylvania began to come into view. I forgot how much I loved the mountains until they began appearing. To me they are home, as is Pennsylvania. It was a beautiful sunny day with blue skies, puffy white clouds, and mile after mile of lush green mountains. The panorama that lay before us was breathtaking.

We had a most enjoyable ride home, talking, remembering all

that we had seen and done, and singing along to the oldies on our CD's. I said to Jim, "This is happiness – a beautiful day, being with you, making an afghan for one of the grandchildren as we ride along, being thankful for the gift we have in each other, and for the many gifts we have in our lives."

We made one stop along the way. Growing up in Philadelphia, Penn State was a revered name. We grew up wanting to see it. We had never been to Penn State; it was on the way home; and we made it the last part of our journey.

Penn State is in the town of State College. The town and the university are beautiful. They are surrounded by mountains on every side. The campus is very large. Between the school, the buildings, the dorms, and the two farms that are also a part of it, it must take up half the town. The football stadium is huge. It was larger than any stadium I have seen. My Uncle Len and my cousin, Joseph, graduated from Penn State and remained loyal to their Alma Mater throughout their lives. They went back to reunions and footballs games as often as they could. It was exciting to finally see Penn State University.

We drove through the town and loved what we saw. The main street is filled with shops and restaurants. The restaurants were so plentiful, we could have had our pick of whatever our taste buds desired that day. The town was packed with people. Many students filled the streets. This was the end of June and they were there for summer courses. Visitors and tourists were also enjoying this beautiful day and the town. I don't think the town of State College is ever dull, no matter what the season.

As we were leaving State College, we drove by a Catholic church. It was aptly named – Our Lady of Victory. Penn State was the victor in so many football games. We made one last stop at this church. We made our three wishes and included prayer intentions. I think it is pretty amazing that our intentions and other's intentions have been carried from church to church across this beautiful country. I am sure prayers helped keep us safe along the way. Thank you, God!

We are now back home in the beautiful little town of Jim Thorpe, Pennsylvania. We have made our permanent home in Florida, but Jim Thorpe will always be our home. We still have a house there. In case you aren't familiar with Jim Thorpe, it is this quaint little town that sits in the foothills of the Pocono Mountains of PA. It is completely surrounded by mountains and is appropriately named, "The Switzerland of America."

Jim Thorpe used to be called Mauch Chunk. The name means "sleeping bear." Looking down from the top of the Flagstaff mountain, the opposite mountain looks like a bear sleeping. It was named that by the Native America Indians who lived in the area before it was populated by immigrants coming from countries all over Europe, but mostly the Irish escaping the potato famine in Ireland. After the demise of the railroad in the area in the 1950's, the townspeople thought that renaming the town after a famous athlete, Jim Thorpe, would bring prosperity to the town. In the 1950's, Mauch Chunk was almost a ghost town, because there weren't any jobs. The townspeople voted to change the name of the town to Jim Thorpe after the famous athlete. They thought that would bring back prosperity because Jim Thorpe was the greatest athlete of his time. However, renaming the town did not bring prosperity. Tourism is what brought prosperity back to the town.

Driving down the mountain road that leads into Jim Thorpe, you would never know there is a town at the bottom of the mountain. Very slowly the Lehigh Gap parts and the town begins to appear as you descend. It is a beautiful sight. The Lehigh River flows at the bottom of the town.

Upon entering the town of Jim Thorpe, you immediately take a step back in time to the Victorian Age. The town is very well preserved. At one time, it was a very affluent railroad town, second only to Niagara Falls in tourism because of the Switchback Gravity Railroad. Eight millionaires lived in the town at one time and their mansions are still there. Asa Packer was one of the millionaires. He was the richest man in the world at his time. His mansion sits high on a hill, for all to see, overlooking the town, and is open for tours. He pioneered and succeeded in transporting coal from the coal mines in the area to the cities by using the railroad. He also built Lehigh University in Bethlehem, Pennsylvania. Asa Packer, coal, and railroading brought prosperity to the town.

Today, prosperity has returned to Jim Thorpe through white-water rafting, bike marathons, several festivals, and the many museums in the town. The town was featured in the 1968 movie, "The Molly Maguires." The Molly Maguires were Irish coal miners who fought for better wages and working conditions in the coal mines. The history of the "Mollies," the Courthouse where they were tried, and the jail where they were hung can also be found in the town and are big attractions to visitors/tourists. The original train station has been preserved. You can meander through the museum at the train station while waiting to go for a ride on the train. The Mauch Chunk Opera House is still open and has many shows throughout the year. My grandmother was in shows at the Opera House when she was young. The many shops, eateries, Victorian homes, and the ambiance of the town make Jim Thorpe a wonderful place for a day trip, weekend getaway, or a vacation. Jim Thorpe was also named one of the most beautiful towns in America. That's a great incentive for a visit!

In case you haven't guessed, I love this town! It is a big part of my roots. My grandmother was born and raised here in the 1880's. My mother spent every summer here with her mother's family. She was happy to be away from the coal mines. I spent every summer here with my grandparents. I was happy to be away from the city. My parents retired to Jim Thorpe and my children spent summer vacations here. Now, my grandchildren come every summer to the house in Jim Thorpe for their vacations. They love it here and tell me, "Granny, you can never sell this house."

I have great memories of my time with my grandparents and now I am making great memories with my grandchildren. Family, history, tradition, it doesn't get any better than this. It is wonderful. By the way, did I mention – I LOVE THIS TOWN?!!!

So, Jim and I are home. It was a fantastic trip. I will miss seeing new and exciting things every day. I will miss having Jim all to myself, talking to each other, laughing at our silly jokes, and singing along to our favorite songs. However, it is good to be in my own home, my own bed, have my family and friends close-by, and to look forward to this summer filled with our grandchildren's joy, laughter, and adventures.

P.S. Dorothy was right, "There's no place like home."

Pennsylvania – **The Keystone State**
State Motto – Virtue, Liberty, and Independence
Keystone State
License Plate Saying

Epilogue

What, you may ask, have I learned from my travels across this beautiful country? In answer I would tell you that I learned that Christianity and God are still very much alive in America. I learned that patriotism and love are still equally alive. I learned that our forefathers and the history of this country is what gave us our greatness and made us the shining star that we are among nations. I learned that our people, Americans, are kind, loving, helpful, friendly, and for the most part, happy people.

I met many people in our travels across this country. They were kind and loving in wishing us well, even praying for our safety. They were helpful and friendly in suggesting places to go and see, even giving us detailed directions on how to get there – and most of all, answering all our questions. People were happy in that they enjoyed their lives, cherished our great country, thankful that they lived here, and were content with their lives.

I hear many Americans talking about going abroad and that is wonderful. I have been to Ireland and Italy and enjoyed my time in both countries. However, I would suggest that Americans see the United States also. I would suggest that they steep themselves in our history, our struggles, our values, and our beauty. After doing that, one can't help but come away with a greater appreciation of our country; one can't help but say, "God Bless America."

Jim and I came away from this trip filled with an incredible love of the United States of America and such gratitude that we live in this wonderful country. Thank you for taking this journey with us. It was nice having you along.

I now pass the torch on to you. Let your journey begin. Try it! Go!! I promise you won't regret it.

Happy Travels!

Made in the USA
Middletown, DE
23 December 2018